CROSS-CULTURAL MARRIAGE
A CHRISTIAN PERSPECTIVE

Branford Yeboah

New Generation **Publishing**

Acknowledgments

This book is dedicated to my granddaughters Precious and Princess. Although I have other grandchildren, the two grand children named above form the basis of this book. They are both mixed-race as a result of cross-cultural marriage. They are the apple of my eye and I take great delight in them. Watching them grow is the greatest thing to have happened to me. They are the inspiration behind this book. I also thank my wife Mary who worked tirelessly in the compilation of some of the materials in this book and also contributed to the book herself. Without her, this book would not have been completed. I also want to thank Emma Ashwood for her brilliant work in the editing of this book.

CONTENTS

INTRODUCTION

This book is aimed at both Christians and non-Christians or those without a faith. The main aims of writing this book are;

1. To warn Christians about the dangers of marrying outside the community of the Christians faith
2. To advise Christians on what to look for when it comes to cross-cultural marriage.
3. To warn people living in our multicultural society about problems that comes with cross-cultural marriage.
4. Some of the customs and traditions you need to know before marriage.

There is nothing wrong in marrying someone from a different culture. The only problem is when you know nothing about the culture of your spouse. Let's take this as an example: you are an English woman without a faith and you fall in love with a Muslim man and the relationship ends in marriage. The question you must ask yourself is what do you know about Islam? What are the views of Islam when it comes to marriage? How does Islam see women in marriage? What does Islam say about divorce? What is a woman's fate in divorce? You have no faith and yet you are married to someone with faith. How do expect the children to be brought up? Or for example, you were born into a religion; does this make you a faithful follower of that religion? Being born into a religion does not make a person committed to it. It takes personal experience before a person can become committee to its beliefs, a Christian who marries someone from another faith cannot claim to be committed to the Christian faith. Let's take another example you are married to someone who is totally committed his or her religion. The stakes here are very high. You are in a relationship because of love and yet you may not know enough about the culture and the religion of the person you have married or what his or her religion would be expecting of you.

To begin with, you are so blinded by love that you could not consider obstacles to marrying someone from a different culture or what their religion will ask of you. Knowing something about the culture of your fiancé will give you a head start when cultural problems start showing up later in the marriage. Familiarizing yourself with your fiancé's culture will help you in times of cultural differences in your marriage. Cross-cultural marriage does not involve love alone; it also involves the culture of each spouse and the behaviour patterns of his or her customs and traditions.

In a world where people marry for different reasons it is difficult to analyze and formulate what each person means by love. For example, the Greek have three words for "love" (agape, Philos and Eros). The English has only one word. A lot of factors come into play before two people can make up their minds as to whether they are compatible. Love is like a catalyst that makes things happen quickly, but marriage needs culture and religion to make it work effectively. To marry on the basis of love alone is like a leap into a deep ocean. We have no idea what the future will be like or how to cope with the uncertainty that comes with it. In cross-cultural relationship, love alone is not enough you need cultural similarities to consolidate the relationship.

The reason that so many cross-cultural marriages are breaking down are because couples from different cultures who are in love do not take a keen interest in studying each others culture and religious beliefs. In a cross-cultural marriage couples who do not address the issues of culture and religion by educating themselves in their spouse's culture are likely to face problems later in the marriage. Those who think culture does not and should not play any significant role in the marriages will one day wake up to find that the very thing they regarded as insignificant is the thing that killed their marriage.

You will never know the profound effect that culture and religion have on marriage until they start to influence it. In considering a cross-cultural marriage, it is imperative that couples in a committed relationship take time to study each other's culture and gather information on the person they plan to marry. Investigating and learning about your fiancé's culture is a good idea. Grandmother once said this about cross-cultural marriage, "It is very important that you know his or her culture thoroughly before committing yourself."

Young men and women in the church and outside the church are making many mistakes when it comes to choosing life partners in cross-cultural relationship. These mistakes are being committed for the following reasons.

1. **Lack of Biblical understanding:** Biblical understanding of marriage is very important for our youth today. It is the responsibility of the Church to teach the youth what the Bible says about marriage and how to live marriage life according to its teaching. The teaching of

Biblical principles on marriage does not end with wedding but continues after marriage. It is not surprising that marriage seldom forms part of the sermon coming from the pulpit.

2. **Spiritual discernment:** How we discern the truth of dreams, visions, prophecies and speaking tongues is very crucial in detecting what the Holy Spirit is saying and what false spirits are saying concerning you and the person you are about to marry.

3. **Decisions and choice:** In a world where deception has become part of some people's lifestyles, it is the responsibility of the Church and Christian parents to lead the youth through the guidance of the Holy Spirit to make good decisions in the choice of their life partners.

4. **Bible and culture:** Culture plays a very significant role in marriage. While some cultures conflict with Biblical principles, others do not. An understanding of your fiancée's culture in the light of Scripture is necessary to avoid confrontations. When two people are in love and come from different cultures it imperative that they study each other's culture thoroughly.

5. **Cross-cultural marriage:** Scriptures does not forbid cross-cultural marriage, except where such marriage can lead either of the spouses into the worship of foreign gods or the worship of spirits.

6. **Cross-religious marriage:** The Scriptures explicitly speaks against such marriage. It is a forbidden pasture from which a Christian may seek out a bride or bridegroom.

Marriage must never be restricted along cultural lines because God created human beings as equals irrespective of the culture we were born into. The coming of Jesus Christ broke down all cultural barriers to liberate everyone under cultural bondage. Therefore, if a person becomes a Christian, he is no longer under any cultural yoke that place a ban on cross-cultural marriage. In Christ we are one, both spiritually and culturally, therefore we are not divided by culture.

Against this, culture should not be allowed to restrict the Christian from choosing to marry only from within his or her culture. Since the Scriptures do not place a ban on cross-cultural marriage, we are powerless to stand against it. Even great men like Abraham, Moses and Solomon all married women from a different culture. However, it must be noted that in the case of Abraham there was an exception in his relationship with Hagar.

It is surprising that there are some Christians who forbid their children from marrying someone from a different culture. Nevertheless, we have to be mindful of certain culture that some Christians are born into, in which women are treated as inferiors. Be on the lookout because some Christians have never grown out of their culture.

Cross-cultural marriage can bring the better of two cultures together. However, we have to be very careful of certain cultures. Although some people have been saved by Christ, they are still married to their culture and hold tightly to their cultural believes. There is nothing morally wrong with this, as long as it does not affect the relationship.

CROSS – CULTURAL COMMUNICATION

Communicating is very important to each culture. Every culture sets rules for the way thoughts and feelings can be communicated politely. For example, it is not just what we say that is important, how we say it is equally important. It is not just what we say that is important. What we do is equally important. Our body language may also affect how our communications are received. All the above are bound up together in the way people communicate within and across cultures.

A key problem associated with communication is that often messages are complex and indirect. In such instances, message may be hidden or misunderstood. This leads to ineffective communication. To be effective, communication must be simple and direct. This means it clearly expresses the intent and purpose of the communication. There is nothing left unsaid or below the surface.

For example, let's look at Proverbs 26:22-26. It says: "The words of a gossip are like choice morsels; they go down to a man's inmost parts. Like a coating of glaze over earthenware are fervent lips with an evil heart. A malicious man disguises himself with his lips, but in his heart he harbours deceit. Though his speech is charming, do not believe him, for seven abominations fill his heart. His malice may be concealed by deception, but his wickedness will be exposed in the assembly."

The Scripture talks about disguising the truth with the lips. This describes complex or complicated

11

communication. There are hidden messages that are not clearly communicated. In fact, below the surface are destructive aspects to the communication.

Sometimes we use techniques in communication that keep us from talking about things as they really are. Some of these are generalizations like "everyone", "nobody," or "always;" assumptions like "I know what he thinks or what he will say," and absolutes like "never" or "this is the way it is." When we do this, our communications are less effective. Look at Proverbs 26: 4. It says "Do not answer a fool according to his folly, or you will be like him yourself."

In verses 18 and 19 of the same chapter we read, "Like a madman shooting firebrands or deadly arrows, is the man who deceives his neighbour and says, "I was only joking." Effective communication is characterized by trust. This involves a level of communications that goes beyond the surface. It is trusting so much that one is wiling to share needs, feelings and experiences from his inner self or life.

In effective communication, both persons must trust each other. I must trust you before I share deep, personal feelings and attitudes with you. I will not share with a person I do not know, because I cannot be sure that such a person will not ridicule me or gossip about me. It is risky to share feeling and attitudes. Therefore, most people tend to talk at levels where there is little or no deep information shared.

Know Your Weaknesses: knowing yourself includes knowing both your strengths and weaknesses. It is especially important to know your weaknesses in order that you may develop strategies for turning your poor communication into a good communications in your marriage. Some common weaknesses of communications are;

1. A vocabulary that is too limited.
2. The inability to pronounce words.
3. Faulty grammar and sentence construction.

Understandably, these weaknesses frequently occur in cross-cultural communications because a spouse is learning a second language. However, they can also learn when a spouse speaks his native vocabulary by systematically studying the meaning of unfamiliar words and begin to use these words in speaking.

In cross-cultural communications some spouses are often handicapped by their inability to express themselves in a clear and precise way. This makes communication very difficult. What we say and how we say it can sometimes affect our communications. However, knowing what you want to say to your spouse and how you say it will give a sense of confidence.

An excellent way to establish good cross-cultural communication is to show enthusiastic interest and concern that is based on understanding. Sometimes in cross-cultural communication the use of good illustrations can be very effective.

The following are some things that contribute greatly to the strength and weaknesses of cross-cultural communications are;

1. **Purpose for communicating:** We must get the right attention of our spouse, because without his or her attention you cannot go further in the communications.
2. **Manner of communicating:** Make sure your spouse is interested in what you have to say and he or she have time to listen what you have to

say. There is no point trying to engage your spouse in communications when he or she has something else to do. For example, he or she is running late to work, has something to do, tired, sick, busy with doing something else, or has no interest in what you have to say. The principal ideas in communication is that it must be presented clearly and logically

3. **Attitude:** What you have to say must be desirable so that he or she wants to know more. Communications must produce thoughts and interest.

4. **Subject:** He or she must be convinced of your sincerity. Is the motive of the subject to gain our own interest or the interest of your spouse? Human beings are so complex; we must examine our motive very carefully so that there are not of our own selfish interest.

Each person has three selves: *the ideal self, the public self, and the real self:* **The ideal self** is what we would like to be. If there are unfavourable difference between our self-image and our ideal self, we may suffer anxiety or guilt, or we may even hate ourselves. Because our ideal is related to our sense of right and wrong, it resists change.

The public self: is the way our spouse see us or others see us. It determines our reputation. We want our spouse to believe certain things about us. We want to be love and appreciated by our spouse.

The real self: consist of his or her inner or deepest feelings, needs and thoughts.

In his book *Communicating Christ Cross-Culturally* David Hesselgrave included the following example to illustrate the importance of language: "**The ambiguity**

of one word may have drastically changed the history of the twentieth century. The Japanese word mokusatsu has two distinct meanings: (1) to ignore, (2) to refrain from comment."

During July 1945 a significant number of influential Japanese people and the Emperor among them- were prepared to consider terms for ending the war with the Allies. The Potsdam ultimatum called for a response from Japan but the Japanese wanted more time to discuss terms. A press release announced that the official cabinet policy was one of **mokusatsu,** and the intended meaning of the word was **"to refrain from comment."**

In the process of translation, however, the foreign press overlooked the **"no comment"** possibility and reported that the Japanese policy was **"to ignore"** the ultimatum. At that point Japanese psychology came into play. The release could have been recalled and restated. That would have involved an admission that entailed a great loss of face, however, and therefore was unthinkable to Japanese leaders.

The **"ignore"** meaning was allowed to stand. Consequently, the voices of reason were not heard and the war continued. Had a settlement been made at that time there would have been no Hiroshima, no Nagasaki, no Russian intervention in Manchuria and (quite possibly) no division of Korea and no Korean War. Tens of thousands of lives might have been saved.

From the above we conclude that meaning is not purely derived from the person speaking, rather the listener takes the words and assigns meaning to it. Meanings are the pure ideas and feeling that exist in a person's mind. However, the meanings you have within you cannot be transferred to another's mind without some change or corruption. People who are married to a husband or wife with a different language will have to be mindful of their choice of words when communicating.

Communication produces the following things in marriage (a) understanding (b) misunderstanding (c) agreement (d) disagreement (e) harmony (f) disharmony (g) satisfaction (h) dissatisfaction (i) happiness (j) unhappiness (k) Reckless Words (l) Pleasant Words (m) Unpleasant Words (n) Rejection (o) Life and Death.

Words can be interpreted differently which is why we have to be cautious in the way we phrase things when communicating. For example, a word considered polite in one culture may be considered impolite in a different culture. Couples in cross-cultural marriages must take a keen interest in the study of their spouse's language to avoid the use of words they may consider offensive.

The problem can be made more complicated where spouses speak different languages or cannot speak each other's language, so they adopt a foreign language that is common to them. For example, a family friend who is Romanian is married to a French man. Neither of them can speak the other's native language, but they both speak English.

English has become the medium of communication in this cross-cultural marriage. Even here, both of them have to be careful in the choice of words because English, their adoptive language, is not their first language. When a language is not your first language, culturally you lack the historical meaning of certain words.

Respect for language is very important in cross-cultural marriage. It is wrong to look down on your spouse's culture, customs and tradition as inferior to yours. You find trouble in your marriage the moment

you start looking down on your spouse language. Language is a gift of God given to man, the crown of His creation, as a medium of communication. Therefore we must respect each other's language or dialect.

Our language is our culture and we are all proud of it. However, in cross-cultural marriages a husband or wife should desist from using his or her dialect as a weapon of gossip when he or she does not want their spouse to understand what is being communicated with a friend or relative.

Never speak a language in the presence of your spouse or in-laws which they cannot speak or understand. The speaking of a language that is unfamiliar in the matrimonial home can send conflicting messages. This can make your spouse believe you are saying something about him or her which you do not want him or her understand. Besides, it is bad manners.

Frequent speaking in a foreign language on the phone or with a relative can spell trouble in the marriage and should be avoided, except where the language being spoken is translated. Couples involved in cross-cultural marriages should summon the courage to tell their friends and relatives that speaking a language that is not familiar to their spouse in the marital home is not allowed.

Let me illustrate a case example for clearer understanding. A couple came to see me about problems they were facing in the marriage. During the conversation, when the wife realized that we both spoke the same language she immediately started speaking in our cultural dialect. This did not help the conversation so the husband insisted his wife speak in English.

Because English was not her first language, she felt better expressing herself in her own language. This made her husband very uncomfortable because he could not understand her. It is very irritating to sit down with someone you have a dispute with while they are speaking in a language you do not understand. Having to wait patiently for someone to do the translation can be a strain.

Translation deals with encoding and decoding a message. A translator without a good command of both languages can cause serious problems. The reason is simple; a word can have multiple meaning and it will be the translator's decision to choose the appropriate meaning of a word. This is where things can go wrong.

The husband wanted to hear exactly what the wife was telling me instead of having her words translated. Here he was right, because in the process of translation, certain words may be lost or wrongly translated. Attaching incorrect meaning to a word is one of the common problems in communication. I told the wife that, in order to have a good discussing and to be fair to her husband she would have to stop communicating in our dialect. It took a lot of persuasion to bring her in line with a language that was common to both of them. I perfectly understood why the wife wanted to express herself in her own language. It is obvious that when a husband or wife is without a good command of the spouse's language, he or she is likely to be misunderstood.

In a cross-cultural marriage, every word spoken should be communicated in the language that is common to the husband and wife. Remember, one of the marks of a good marriage is **transparency**.

The safe rule in cross-cultural communication is to avoid communicating in a language your spouse cannot understand. A person who cannot understand the words being spoken watches the body language of the speaker and then assigns meaning to them. The listener's reactions are then based on the meaning assigned to the speaker's gestures and expressions.

Words can be hurtful if not properly used in cross-cultural marriage. This is the reason why in communication we must try to use words that are not ambiguous. What we must remember is that meaning does not come only from the person encoding the message but also with the person decoding the message.

When a person is speaking, it the listener who creates their own understanding of what the speaker is saying. For example, you may say something with an intended meaning, but the listener will decode the meaning different from yours. A troublemaker can easily hide behind the ambiguity of a word and assign a meaning that is contrary to yours.

Things to consider: You need to consider the beliefs and values that exist in your in-law's culture. In cross-cultural communication, in-laws are very particular about the manner of speech and how they are addressed. The manner in which you communicate with your in-laws will help to make you acceptable or unacceptable.

Culturally, communication reveals much about our attitude and behaviour which enables in-laws to assess whether you accept their culture or you are willing to learn about the culture you have married into. In-laws can take particular delight when communicating with daughter in-laws or son-in-laws from different cultures.

It will amaze you that communicating with in-laws will reveal things about you of which are not aware. For example, things like your acceptance of their culture and your views about them will make them feel welcome or unwelcome. What you should remember is that in cross-cultural marriage we communicate culturally. This means your communication should not offend your spouses' culture.

In cross-cultural marriage, culture and ethnic background play a significant role in the beliefs and values of your in-law's customs and traditions. When communicating, you should not consider your spouse's culture as inferior to your culture just because it is different.

In-laws appreciate daughters-in-law or son-in-law who appreciate their culture and want to be part of it. By being part of your wife's or husband's culture does not strip you of your own cultural heritage. Remember, everyone's roots are buried in his or her culture and nothing can change that. When communicating culturally you should consider the **social customs** of your in-laws. This is all important because customs and tradition dictates a person's culture.

Some cultures from Africa or the Middle East attach so much importance to words. When communicating with your in-laws, be mindful of the words you chose. Mannerism is a particular way of speaking or behaving that the person may not be aware. In Cross-cultural communication it is very important for two reasons (a) habits and (b) behaviour.

In Asia, Africa and the Middle East courtesy in communication is a reflection of good manners. In some cultures it is imperative that a person of a lower rank communicate courteously to a person of a higher rank. However, in the Western world this may not be so, because certain words that may appear offensive to a person coming from Asia or Africa may not be so to a Westerner.

Spouses coming from different cultural backgrounds have to be extra-careful when communicating with in-laws or members of each other's families. We have nothing to loose by being courteous in our communications. In an attempt to break cultural communication barriers, the key word we must remember is courtesy.

When communicating with your in-laws from a different cultural background it is best to look directly at them because it convinces them of your sincerity. If you fail to do this, it gives them the impression that you are insincere. If your in-laws are convinced of your sincerity, then you have begun to win them over. This then becomes the binding cord that will hold the two cultures together.

Eye contact is another important factor in cultural communication for the following reasons:

1. A good eye contact indicates you are interested in the conversation.
2. Eye-contact indicates the right attitude irrespective of the cultural differences.
3. Eye-contact stimulates feedback from your in-laws. It can also reveal if they are interested in the conversations.
4. Eye-contact convinces your spouse of your sincerity.
5. Good eye-contact helps in to get a feedback.
6. Can make you know whether your spouse is interested, bored, confused or angry.

Communication differs from culture to culture. For example, in Niger, when Wodaabe people greet each other, they may not look each other directly in the eye. Greetings in this manner is localised within the Wodaabe people alone. When you move from their culture into other cultures within Niger it is quite different.

In Africa, Asia, Middle East and the Far-East face-saving in communication is very important, especially where it involves a person of senior rank and a person of junior rank. In some cultures, people of junior rank must show humility and submission when communicating with a person of a higher authority, e.g. between father and son or an elder and a youth.

Things to avoid in communication: Speaking in a language your in-laws do not understand must be avoided completely. For example, speaking with your sister or brother in a language your in-laws do not understand can cause a lot of problems.

By observing the movement of the mouth and eyes a person who cannot understand your language will visualise what you are saying although, his or assumption may be wrong. The danger here is that the listener may read the wrong meaning into your words.

As you speak, you choose words to convey your meaning. At the same time, facial expressions, gestures, and tone of voice all nonverbal cues accompany your words and affect the meaning that your listener receives. The listener takes both the verbal symbols and the nonverbal cues and assigns meanings to them. One of the major causes of trouble in cross-cultural marriages can be attributed to ambiguities in communication.

It is through communication that we express our aspirations, goals, and the evaluations of what we have done in our marriage, what we have achieved and the direction we want our marriage to go. Communications plays a crucial role in our marriage. In communication, many married couple verbalise demands for themselves, which are completely unrealistic. Perhaps this contributes to the high rate of marital problem and divorces in so many marriages. Some married couples distort their own identities by harmful way they describe themselves: **"I'm lazy"**; **"I'm ugly"**; **"I'm just not good and would never be"**, **"I'm nothing but a failure."** These expressions do not help us to be worthwhile husbands or wives in the marriage.

In marriage communications we must properly evaluate ourselves first by knowing ourselves, then by being ourselves. After we do this, we can present our best self by accurate, positive, and persuasive self-expression in communicating with our spouses. *Above this, we need the help of the Holy Spirit to improve our self-expression in order to be effective communicators in our marriage.*

UNDERSTANDING YOUR SPOUSE'S CULTURE

Cultural assimilation is very important in cross-cultural marriage for three reasons.

1. It helps to bridge the gap between the two cultures.
2. It enhances a cultural world-view.
3. Cultural behaviour: the first step in understanding your spouse's culture is by understanding your own culture. Without this, you cannot link the two cultures together.

As you consider the significance of the culture you were born into, it opens your eyes to certain behavioural patterns within your culture that you may not be aware of. You may find out that certain types of behaviour in your culture are not acceptable to you. Until we fully understand our own culture, we will find it difficult to accept others' culture.

People who look down on others' culture do so because they do not understand their own cultural worldview. For example, Kevin, an Englishman is married to Asantewaa, a Ghanaian. After the wedding, they went to Ghana for their honeymoon. Throughout their stay, he noticed people eating with their hands. This observation surprised him, and he asked why they do not eat with cutlery.

Sometimes it is difficult to understand certain things about others' culture until we look into our own culture. This happens when we are enveloped in our own cultural capsule. Only by then will we understand why other cultures eat with their hands. In certain cultures the type of food determines whether they eat with the hand, fork and knife, chopsticks or with a spoon.

The ways people behave differ from one culture to another for example; the way and manner people talk. A behaviour patterns reflects a person's culture. In cross-cultural marriage we need to understand how our spouses feel about certain things in our culture, the way we behave culturally and the way we think culturally. There are certain behaviour patens which is very noticeable among certain cultures.

What is regarded as right and wrong in one culture cannot be assumed to be applicable to another culture. What is right and what wrong in every culture is dictated by that culture and therefore cannot be regarded as a universal way of doing things. However, there are certain ways of doing things that are universally accepted as the norm and can be linked culturally.

For example, in some African countries, custom has it that an older person is always right, it does not matter if he or she is at fault. If there is a dispute and the elder person is at fault, the person settling the dispute must find a way to tell him or her so and impose a suitably mild fine on the person of lower rank without openly stating that the older person is in the wrong. This may not be culturally right in the West. A Westerner intending to marry an African should take note of this.

In a Western society an older person can be told in the presence of a younger person he or she has offended that he is wrong without any bad feeling from the older person. **Face-saving** is very important to people from Africa and Asia. It is intertwined in the very fabric of the African and Asian customs and traditions. It is said that the customer is always right; similarly in the African tradition the older person is always right.

For example, if a father has a dispute with his son and the father is at fault. This pose a dilemma for the judge who have to find a way of pronouncing the father not guilty, and at the same time find a means of imposing a fine on the son that will not make him look guilty.

Status and role: Status is essentially the social position assigned to an individual, his or her place on the social ladder. With regard to a person's status, certain expectations, beliefs, and sentiments are attached; this determines the role of the individual. Role is the function or position that a person has or is expected to have.

Therefore, those crossing their cultural boundary to marry would have to ask themselves these questions (1) who I am in relation to my spouse's culture? (2) Who are my spouse's family in relation to my culture? In some cultures, to fail to communicate according to the status of the family members may be regarded as disrespect.

Social structure: This includes family, extended family, and clan. The criterion for identifying social structure is that relationships growing out of it are of critical importance. Let's use a West African proverb for the purpose of explanation. The proverb says: "You look after a baby while he grows teeth and he looks after you when you lose yours." This is about the nearest English translation. In Africa, Asia, the Middle East and South and Central America families bring children into the world so that the children will look after them when they are old. This is one of the reasons why people from such countries tend to have more children. They regard children as investment.

Against this, they guard the children jealously and will do anything to have unrestricted accesses to their investment. This method of family investment causes many marital problems. For example, after investing so much time and money educating a son or daughter to college or university, they expect something in return once their son or daughter starts working.

When a family sells a parcel of land to educate a son or send a son or daughter overseas, they expect something in return. I will use a good friend's experience as an illustration. After graduating, his parents sent him to London to further his education. On completion of his education, he got a lucrative job working for an investment bank.

After working for one year, his wife joined him in London without the knowledge of his parents. The sudden disappearance of his wife raised suspicions among the families. When the family got to know that his wife had joined him it provoked anger because they felt he should have invited one of his brothers instead of his wife.

After three years he brought over one of his children. The family branded him as selfish and insensitive to the plight of the family who toiled to get him where he is. The family sent him a five-page letter reminding him of his duty to the family. Some of his brother made threatening phone calls.

Taking his remaining two children out of the country to join him in London was the last straw that finally severed the relationship between him and his brothers. Despite this, he still supports the family financially but this was not enough as long as he was not helping his brothers to join him in London.

His wife became the subject of verbal attacks; they blamed her and held her responsible for not allowing her husband to at least get one of his brothers to London. His wife was called all sorts of names and told she was nothing but a wedge that has caused the progress of the family wheel to grind to a halt. It is quite natural in some cultures for the family to blame their son's wife for whatever goes wrong in the marriage.

These are some of the problems facing people who come from a culture that regard their children as family investment. In such cultures the wives are always in the line of fire. The wife is blamed for everything that prevents their son from bankrolling the family. They see their son as a fruit-bearing tree they should be the first to eat from.

A West African adage goes like this, "A woman goes into a marriage to bring wealth to the family, however, if the wife incurs debt it the husband's responsibility." This could be one of the reasons why parents seem to be over-protective of their son's. If parents know a marriage could deprive them of their investment they will derail the relationship by citing cultural differences or finding faults with the fiancé's culture.

Family interference is one of the greatest contributing factors in divorce, as evidenced by high level of family interferences in their son or daughter's marriage. The reason for this is each parent is seeking their son or daughter's interest. The likely scenario here is that the wife's parents are only interested in what their daughter can get out of the marriage. Meanwhile, the husband's family try to stop their son from offering unnecessary financial assistance to the wife's family.

The scenario described above is peculiar to Africa, Asia and the Middle East and really not a problem in

Europe or North America. Westerners who have married into these cultures or those looking to marry from these cultures must be aware of this as an issue that can turn a happy marriage into a marriage that could be marred by cultural differences. This has caused a lot of marital problems with men who are married to Western women.

In multicultural society, understanding the culture of your fiancé is the first step before committing yourself. The second step is to know much about the person and the third step is to find out as much as possible about his culture, customs, traditions, his family and extended families. You can do this by obtaining information's from the library or from the internet.

You can also obtain information from the cultural centre or through the embassy of your fiancé or fiancée's country. Information gathered from such sources could help prepare you before marrying someone whose culture is different from yours. In cross-cultural marriage it is best to be fully prepared and aware of a culture you about to be exposed to through marriage. It is a tragic mistake that so many people are blinded by the love that they fail to see pitfalls in some cross-cultural marriages.

You are from South America and you live in London. You met and fell in love with a young man from Africa. You married and promised each other that England would be your adopted country. Then after eight years of marriage with three children your husband drops this bombshell; "I want to go back to my country and settle down." What would be your answer to this statement? Do you see yourself betrayed by the person who promised to honour the pre-marriage agreement?

Would you be willing to go with him? If the answer is yes, then how prepared are you? Do you know what awaits you? Do you know much about the country, its people and their culture which is about to become your new home and part of your life? Did you ever think of this before you married him? Or did you think it would never happen?

Women who have adequately prepared themselves by learning their husband's culture will have no problem settling down in their husband's culture. On the other hand, women who have not studied their husband's culture will resist such a move to a culture that is different to their own. These are some of the pitfalls women in cross-cultural marriages will be confronted with one day, and will have to come to terms with. It is going to happen one day, except where both spouses were born in the same cosmopolitan society and come from different cultures.

For example, if you are an English woman, married to an Asian man born in Britain, you don't have to worry whether one day your husband will want to settle in the country where his parents came from because that probability is very remote. However, if you get married to an Asian man not born in Britain then the probability is very high. If your fiancé or your husband tells you that he has no intention of going back to his country of birth, do not believe him.

Western women, who are engaged or are in relationships with men from different cultures who were born in Africa, Asia, the Middle East or South America, who are concerned that their future spouse may relocate to their country of birth, need to talk with their fiancé concerning their fear before they make any commitment. The truth is that men who were born outside the Western society and are married to Western women are more likely go back to their country of birth when the reason for which they came to the Western country is achieved.

On the other hand, children who were born to migrant parents in Western countries are unlikely to relocate to their parent's country of birth. Therefore, Western women who are in cross-cultural relationship and are worried of one day following their husband to his country of birth should find out where their boyfriend or fiancé was born.

Let's take another example. If you are South American woman living in London and fall in love with a man from Asia, the Middle East or Africa and you do not intend to go and live in the birth country of your fiancé then you would be better off looking for men from these countries who were born in the United Kingdom in other to avoid being told one day they want to relocate to their country of birth. However, if this is not a problem for you, then you can go ahead and marry him.

Universities and colleges where students from different countries come to study are the breeding ground for cross-cultural marriages. Some students fall in love, and marry without investigating each others culture, because culture means nothing to them. One look at a marriage ceremony and you will see that marriage is engraved in culture.

Generally, Western women are very adaptive and as such more likely to settle in their husband's country and blend in without problems than women from other countries. This is because they are more likely to study the culture of their spouse and willing to adapt.

In Africa, Asia and the Middle East countries, first born children are expected to be the breadwinner of the family when the father is not around. Therefore, the pressure on them to settle at home is greater than the other siblings. First born sons in some culture come under enormous pressure to marry from their own culture to ensure their commitment to the family. Being a first born son in some cultures comes with huge responsibilities. Western women who are dating men from these continents will have to take keen interest in knowing what role the man they are dating holds in the family.

Failure to do this can lead to unexpected problems in the marriage; for example, what if after years of marriage you discover your spouse is heir to the throne in his home town. And he is being summoned by the kingmakers to come and ascend to the throne due to the demise of his father. What will you say to your husband? Go with him or prevent him from ascending to the throne?

A friend once said, "If because of love, we reject what culture regard as the norm in cross-cultural marriage and try to redefine our own pattern for cross-cultural marriage then we will reap the tragic consequences. Never let yourself be lulled into thinking that what culture regards as the norm in cross-culture marriage doesn't matter."

Do you know that in some countries along the west coast of Africa when a husband dies the wife will have to sleep with her husband's corpse for a whole night? What would you do if are a European woman or woman from a country where such customs are not practised? Would you consent and go through an ancient ritual that has outlived it usefulness.

Do you know that in some African countries, when the husband dies the wife has to shave her head and walk barefooted throughout the mourning period? Do you know that in some countries when the husband dies the wife will have wear black dress for a whole year? Do you know that in some culture when the husband dies everything he owned goes to his brothers?

Do you know that in some cultures along the West Coast of Africa when the husband dies, it is his sister's children (nephews) who inherit his property and not his own biological children? The reason for this is that the blood of the family flows in the vein of the female's children and not the male children. In this culture, women in the family produce the heir to a throne and not the men. For example, when a king dies, it is not his son who will ascend to the throne, bur rather one of his sister's children. According to their custom, the royal blood flows through the veins of the king's sister's children and not the king's wife, therefore king's children are not qualified to ascend to the throne.

Space will not allow me to write some of the despicable things some cultures put women through when their husband dies. In some cultures when the husband dies his wife also dies with him, and she is forgotten. It is the husband's family who take control of the husband's estate and she is effectively ruled out of the husband's property.

Some families go beyond this by stripping the wife of everything she had worked to achieve with the husband. To add insult to injury, she is driven out her matrimonial home and told to go to her parents' home. In some cultures, where there are no children, the wife is not even recognised as having married their son, as soon as the husband dies.

Do know that in some cultures women are treated as slaves. Women simple do not have any rights therefore they are hardly consulted in an issue that concerns the family. In this kind of culture once the woman is married to the man she becomes the man's property. A man who comes from a culture that regards women as property may not need her permission before taking certain decisions.

Men from this kind of culture can beat their wives to pulp at the slightest provocation. Men who beat their wives are possessed by an evil spirit and therefore need to be delivered. A man in his right man will never beat the woman he loves. Deliverance through the Power of the Holy Spirit is the only way out and not through therapy. Therapy cannot cast a demon out of a person.

The use of therapy to cure or deliver a husband who beats his wife at the slightest provocation is the wrong approach to towards deliverance and restoration. A violent husband is like a man possessed by a demonic spirit and a counsellor will be wasting his or her time trying to help him overcome his evil behaviour.

Spiritual things needs spiritual solution and physical things needs physical solutions like therapy. To send a man with violent behaviour to a therapist when he is possessed by a demon will only compound the problem. To marry a woman you love so dearly that you chose her above all the women and turn her into a punching bag raises questions about your views of women.

I know of a family friend who will beat his wife at the lightest argument. And when the demon leaves him, he will ask his wife how she sustains her injuries. He will cry and beg his wife for forgiveness. When asked why he beats his wife, he would say, "I don't know what took control over me." Sending such a man to an anger therapy or for counselling will be a waste of time. It is obvious this man's problem is spiritual rather than physical. Husbands who beat their wives are sick and must seek spiritual help.

It is difficult to tell what goes on in the minds of husbands who beat their wives. The most plausible explanation is an evil possession. A loving and caring husband will never show his strength and courage on his defenceless wife. A husband's duty in marriage is to protect his wife both in the home and outside the home, to love and cherish her, and not to subject her to battering by turning her into a punching bag.

The following example is an eyewitness account of a husband who beat his wife and stripped her naked by ripping her dress into pieces in public barely five months after their wedding. This was a woman he vowed to love and cherish when said, "I do." Sometimes I find it hard to understand how some women choose their husbands.

In a moment of madness, this possessed man could not wait for his wife to come home from work to cook for the family. Therefore he decided to go to his wife's office to find out why she was late in coming home. On the way, he saw his wife standing by a taxi she had hired to bring her home, however, the taxi had developed mechanical problem.

In his fit of rage he had no time to ask the taxi driver if there was anything he could do to help. Instead he dragged his wife from among the other passengers waiting for taxis and beat her. Then he walked away proudly back home as if nothing has happened. Surely something did happen, and what happened was that an innocent wife was beaten. When his wife came home, he expected her to cook for the family, which she did, but she did not eat the food. Then the husband went to bed expecting his wife to join him so that he could make love with her. That night she slept with her children. Only a shameless man would beat his wife to pulp and demand sex with her.

This is the way some people live their lives: they hurt others badly and then behave as if nothing has happened. People like this are insensitive to the feelings of those they hurt. All they care about is satisfying the cravings of their inner feeling. Husbands like this leave a trail of battered women as they move from one relationship to the other.

If you are a woman married to a violent man who beats you because he comes from a culture that allows men to beat up their wives, the next time he raises his hands to strike you, tell him, "Beating me will not bring money home. You would be better off beating someone in the boxing ring to bring a lot of money home for the family."

If you feel you are strong and want to test your strength, please do not test it on your defenceless wife. The boxing ring is the most appropriate place for husbands who beat wives to show their strength and courage, and not in the marital home. Every marital home is meant to be peaceful and happy the way God wants it to be. Only a fool will turn it into a boxing ring.

Married men who understand what marriage really means will never beat their wives. A man who understands what it means to love the woman he married will seek her highest interest. If you married your wife because you loved her, then you must be bold and honest to tell her you come from a culture which regards beating women as the norm, so she can make up her mind whether she would be willing to put up with a man who will beat her at the slightest argument. Wife beating does not form part of the marriage vows. Therefore men who enjoy beating their wives desecrate the institution of marriage.

Men who beat their wives are nothing but cowards and only show courage and strength on their defenceless women. Wife-beating is a taboo and breaking this taboo comes with a curse. Nothing should make a loving husband beat his loving wife; even at the extreme of provocation a husband must exercise self-control. Do you love your wife enough to make you jealous if another man looks at her twice? If the answer is yes, then why turn your wife into a punching bag?

We marry a woman to love and cherish and not reduce her to the status of a maid. Even a maid has right which prevent her employer from maltreating her. *Similarly, the marriage vow is a legal document that protects the right of a woman in marriage.* Husbands who beat their wives only succeed in filling their marital homes with toxic chemicals. A home that is clouded with poisonous fumes is a poor environment in which to bring children up. Children watch what daddy is doing to mummy and think wife-beating is part of married life.

Only men and women who have no respect for customs and traditions would blindly walk into cross-cultural marriage thinking everything will be fine because they regard cross-cultural marriage as a trial and error marriage. They would walk out when confronted with storms. People who attach less value to marriage do not care about the culture of the person they are marrying.

Some people really do not care where the person they are going to marry comes from, or about his or her cultural beliefs. Some people also marry from cultures other than their own because they want something different; others marry because they know what it means to be married to someone from different culture.

Do you know that in some cultures when a man marries, the woman not only becomes his property but also the property of his family? Therefore, when the husband dies she may be compelled to marry any of her late husband's brothers. The problem with this custom is made worse where there have not been children in the marriage before the husband died. I know of a Caribbean young woman from the Dominican Republic who met and married a Nigerian man in London. After five years of marriage, her husband decided to move to Nigeria. Four years after they settled in Eastern Nigeria, her husband died. A year after the death of the husband she was confronted with the realities of African culture and customs.

One hot afternoon while she was enjoying the African sun with her children, she was summoned before the elders of her husband's immediate family. The elders told her the purpose of the meeting was to explain the customary rites of a widow. After they explained in detail their customs and traditions, she was speechless, because she simply could not comprehend how to make sense of her husband's strange culture. She found herself alone, confronted with a strange culture without any trusted member of her husband's family she could rely on for advice and thousands of miles from home.

The stakes were very high because she and her husband had invested all their life-savings in a joint business venture in Nigeria. The problem here was that she was not only married to her husband, but also his family. Her husband's family needed a yes or no answer to their proposal, and this young woman had to think very carefully before giving an answer.

In her culture it was unthinkable for a woman to be asked to marry one of her husband's siblings after the husband's demise. Cross-cultural marriage comes with its own problems; just as any other marriage have their own problems.

To say no to the elders of the family would mean walking away from the investment, leaving everything to her husband's relatives. Yes would mean taking control of the entire business and keeping the children. She was young and the possibility of her remarrying was greater than staying single. Therefore, she carefully weighed the merits of marrying within the family and marrying outside the family. In this, she placed the interest of the children above anything else. She thought carefully about the safety and the future security of the children, and then decided it was wealth giving in to the demands of her late husband's family.

If this young Caribbean woman had researched properly the customs of her husband before marriage she would have thought carefully before committing herself into an unknown and strange culture that gave her no choice in the event of her husband's demises.

THE FORBIDDEN MARRIAGE

Conservative traditionalists have lost the fight against cross-cultural marriage in part because they are on the losing side of the culture paradigm in today's multicultural society. If they had reached out to people with whom they have disagreement on the issues of cross-cultural marriage to find a common ground on which they could resolve their differences. Mistake which otherwise could have been avoided now separates some families.

One cold winter night, my wife and were watching a documentary, entitled "In search of stolen children" In this documentary, a young English woman travelled to Pakistan in search of her children. The plight of this young woman drew tears from our eyes. In her quest to bring her children back to England where they belong, she vowed never to give up.

But the battle to get the children back was not going to be easy because the odds were stacked against her for the following reasons: 1 where do they find the children, 2 cultural differences, 3 religious differences and 4. Financial constrain. Nevertheless, the love for her children drove her to sell some of possession to overcome the insurmountable.

This is the story of a young woman who came home from work and found her son and daughter were no where to be found. The children were gone, stolen by paid kidnappers. But this man underestimated the bond that existed between mother and children. She put up a spirited defence to get her children back by travelling to Pakistan.

This woman is not alone. Other women, who are married to men from different faiths or culture, have lost their children. In cross-cultural marriage, women who fail to check their fiancée's culture and religious background are likely to face problems in the marriage. Statistics show such marriages don't work in the interest of Western women. Sometimes it pays to find out your fiancé's cultural background.

Cross-cultural marriage is it a crazy marriage? What do people say and what is your opinion about cross-cultural marriage? Should it be encouraged or discouraged? Are those kicking against this form of marriage wasting their time or do they have a case to prove? If they have a case can they prove it beyond reasonable doubt enough to make others walk away from it? A friend once remarked, "If this trend of cross-cultural marriage is allowed to continue we will end with race-less society and many lost culture."

On the other hand, those who advocate for cross-cultural marriage see it as means of building a future generation **with one people, one race, one language and one culture.** In a world that migration has turned into a global village, the human race cannot stop cross-cultural marriage. Kicking against cross-cultural marriage will bring those for and against it to showdown that will leave both parties in limbo.

Is protecting a pure cultural race a good reason to kick against cross-cultural marriage? If the answer is yes, then the good news is that cross-cultural marriage started from the very day marriage began. The only way to stop cross-cultural marriage is to stop the migration of people. But sorry, it is too late because the purity of the human race has been already contaminated by human migration. Therefore, those who would like to stop cross-cultural marriage can never accomplish their dream.

Migration is the unchangeably fact that has stands in the way of those who oppose cross-cultural marriage. Countries depend on each other to survive in this world, countries trade with each other; countries learn each other language for easy transaction for trade and communication. Countries compete with each other in music festivals, sports and games, for example the Olympic Games and FIFA world cup and other bilateral games. The examples above are what have turned migration into a vehicle that accelerated cross-cultural marriage.

On other hand, wars and civil war have also resulted in mass migrations of people fleeing from their war-torn country into neighbouring countries and beyond for safety. Others flee from tyrants who rule with an iron fist. Drought is another factor that causes mass migration. When people are faced with starvation, they are compelled to migrate to any country where they can find food.

Again, poverty is another factor that contributes to mass migration of people from poorer countries to richer countries. People who migrate on the basis of improving their live hood are termed as economic migrants. This migration takes place when richer countries turn their back to the plight of poorer countries.

These are some of the reasons why we have cross-cultural marriage in a world where people are constantly on the move. From the above we can conclude that, the movement of people are the main reasons for cross-cultural marriage. Multicultural societies are the breeding grounds for cross-cultural marriage.

Let's take a country like the United Kingdom, which is made up of England, Scotland, Wales and Northern Ireland. Each of these countries has different cultures, customs and traditions. They have different language and dialect. These countries have lived side by side for years, yet each of them has maintained their separate identity and culture.

Can anyone prevent cross-cultural marriage among these countries that have formed a union for a peaceful co-existence? In a union like this you will have English marrying Irish and Irish marrying Welsh, again you will find Welsh marrying Scots and Scots marrying English. Free movement of people in these countries forms the basis of cross-cultural marriage.

In a country like the United States of America which is a country of immigrants, you can not prevent cross-cultural marriage no matter how hard certain cultures within the country try to stop such marriages. For example, when you confine a group of people who oppose with those who don't oppose cross-cultural marriage for a long period of time, you will be surprised to see that their opposition and attitude will start to change towards cross-cultural marriage.

The blending of two cultures in a marriage is what makes cross-cultural marriage unique; its uniqueness brings out the better of the two cultures. However, we must be mindful of marrying stranger whose culture is different from ours.

I know of young Ghanaian nurse who met and married a man from Jamaica in London. What the young woman did not know was that this loving and caring husband had a wife in his native Jamaica.

It was only when she and her daughter visited Jamaica for the first time that she discovered the husband lied about his marital status. This story is only the tip of the iceberg. There are numerous stories of how people from different cultures have taken advantage of their innocent spouses for their selfish interest.

If you meet someone you love from a different culture, do not be blinded by love. Before you make any commitment, pause for a moment and ask yourself these questions: "Do I know this man or woman enough to commit my life to him or her. Do I know much about his family and where he or she comes from? Am I satisfied he or she is not committed to someone else in his or her native country?"

Waiting is the litmus test for identifying people who marry for the wrong reasons. To carry out the test is simple; just keep them waiting as long as you can. In their desperation to get married they may expose their reason for the marriage proposal. Your fiancé's reasons for leaving his native country and coming to your country sums up in some cases his or her reasons for marriage.

In most cross-cultural marriages, people marry for various reasons and their reasons are what will one day end the marriage. Like all marriages, some people marry for what they can get out of the marriage.

The problem here is that marriage has no crystal ball you can gaze into and see the end from the beginning so that you can get rid undesirable suitors. If marriage had a crystal ball, some marriages would never have taken place and hearts would never have been wounded. Some people are not honest when it comes to cross-cultural marriage. This is because in most cases their reason for marrying desecrates the spirit of cross-cultural marriage.

Nevertheless, some marry for genuinely reasons and these can be seen in the litmus test of love and submission. When a person wants to marry for the right reasons, he or she can wait as long as it takes. What

44

gives him or her strength and patience to wait is love. Love can wait no matter how long it takes for a person to make up his or her mind.

However, cross-cultural marriage can sometimes be a risky marriage if you come from a family of conservative, or traditionalist, where marrying outside of your culture is taboo. Sometimes cross-cultural marriage can defy the odds and fly high where traditional marriages have failed. Sometimes cross-cultural marriage can enjoy great success and happiness.

However, cross-cultural marriage can face deep disappointments and the haunting reality of failure, leading to heartbreak and you wondering if it was worth going into such a marriage that was opposed from the beginning by traditionalist and conservative members of the family.

A good illustration of this is the story of a young English woman called Claire from a middle class family. At university, she met and fell in love with a young man from North Africa. Three years after graduating they were married against a strong opposition from the conservative members of her family, but she was in no mood to back down.

Seven years of marriage produced three children: two boys and a girl. The marriage waxed strong against the expectations of those who opposed the marriage. Their marriage was a happy cross-cultural marriage that weathered the storms of hard line conservative that saw cross-cultural marriage as something that stood in the way of preserving a pure race.

One cold winter evening, Claire came from work to find that her husband and three children were nowhere to be found. She made several phone calls to all her husband's friends and close relative, without success. Just as she was about to call the police, her attention was drawn to note, poorly written on a dirty envelope that read: "As you read this note the children and I are far away in Egypt. Please do not look for us."

Shocked and heartbroken, she was faced with the reality of cross-cultural marriage. Where and to whom should she turn? She became a laughing stock among those who opposed her marriage from the beginning. And now the man she loved and defied her family to marry has abandoned her and given reason for members of her family who opposed cross-cultural marriage to mock and ridicule her.

Where does she start? Egypt! The thought of her three children inspired her quest to bring them home. With the help of friends she embarked on mission impossible to a culture that had no respect for women and a religion that regards non-members as infidels. If this woman had educated herself in her husband's religion and culture, her story could have been different today.

When this woman embarked on her journey she vowed: "I am not coming home without the children." With the help of an Egyptian friend married to English man she travelled to Egypt in search of her three children. Through the good influence of her friend's family, they were able to track them down and secure the release of the children. Although happy to have her children, she was sad that her marriage did not turn out the way she wanted.

Despite this unfortunate example, it will interest you to know that the majority of cross-cultural marriages work well. Certain cultures are not compatible when it comes to cross-cultural marriage. This woman was highly educated and should have known that when it comes to religion liberals and conservatives do not mix. Yet she being a liberal Christian went ahead and married a conservative Muslim. If this liberal Christian had taken time to examine the cultural and religious background of her husband she would not have been in muddy waters.

The story of Helen is another example of how cultural conservatives and out of-touch traditionalists, can be a stumbling block in the path of couples who are in cross-cultural relationships. Helen is of mixed race; her father is French and her mother a Ghanaian. She was born in Ghana and brought to London to be educated at the age of eleven.

Whilst at school she became attached to an English boy from a middle-class family. After secondary education they both went to the same sixth-form college. Then they went to the same university where she studied Accountancy and he studied Law. All the while, the boyfriend's conservative family found nothing wrong with the relationship.

Then, five years after graduation from university her boyfriend proposed to her. The boyfriend's proposal released the toxic feelings that had been dormant in the members of his conservative family. Who thought the relationship would not go beyond friendship.

When the conservative members of the young man's family realised their worst fears was about to be realised they gang up and opposed the marriage. They told Helen's boyfriend; "You have to choose between the family and your girlfriend."

The hard-line conservatives had drawn the battle lines, and for Helen it was a difficult time. She never thought their marriage would be opposed by the family she grew up to love and imagined she would one day join. What Helen did not know was that publicly they appeared to endorse the relationship, but secretly they wished it had never existed. This reminds me of what grandfather once said: "There are some Christians who publicly oppose the devil and secretly agree with him."

47

When Helen's boyfriend could no longer withstand the stiff opposition from his family and not wanting to break the family apart, he ended the relationship. Disappointed and heartbroken, she waked away feeling betrayed by the only boy she had known in her life. As a result she found it difficult to trust any man again. She turned down all the suitors who came to seek her hand in marriage. Even at the time of writing this book she is still not married.

Families who oppose cross-cultural marriage should examine the feelings of their sons and daughters and reasons why they decided to marry someone from a different culture. The fact that your future son or daughter in-law will be from a different culture than yours is never a good reason to oppose the marriage.

Every parent wants what is best for their children and wants to be part of the decision-making processes to ensure their son or daughter has a happy marriage. However, in trying to be involved in your son or daughter's choice of future husband you must be mindful of their reasons for marrying outside their culture. For some, marriage within their own culture is not appealing so they turn elsewhere for a happy marriage.

As a parent, whatever your reasons are for opposing your daughter or son's decision to marry someone from a different culture, we must be aware that there is no one particular race in this world that can claim the purity of its race. Intermarriage from past generations to the present means all races are mixed. Therefore, conservatives and traditionalists who continue wrangling over cross-cultural marriage race are wasting their time. The merit of cross-cultural marriage far outweighs its demerits. A cross-cultural marriage brings out the uniqueness of two cultures that are concealed to both cultures.

A Turkish friend who is married to English man faced a stiff opposition from the very beginning of their relationship. Her future mother in-law told her she does not look like one of them. So she objected to the relation on the grounds that she could not bring herself to watch her son marry a foreigner. She did not hide her feelings about her future daughter in-law's relationship with her son.

Because of her strong opposition, when the wedding date was fixed she was not invited to the wedding less she spoil the party and they did not tell her where the wedding would be taking place. When the newly married couple returned from the honeymoon, she blamed her daughter in-law for leaving her off the guest list. What she did not know was that the decision not to inform her of the day of the wedding was her son's.

Her mother in-law became a thorn in the marriage. The more she showed her disgust towards her daughter in-law, the more their love for each other waxed strong. When she realised her son would have none of her plan to derail the marriage she started pretending to be nice to her daughter in-law to avoid losing her son.

When the in-laws went to see their first grandson, they went to stay with her. When the baby was brought from the hospital, the mother in-law took the baby in her arms and exclaimed "I do not think this is Jason's son because he is not white enough!" From the beginning she was never happy about the marriage, and this was her ignorant way of publicly making her views known.

When it comes to marriage what matters is happiness and not where a man or woman comes from or what he or she looks like. The colour of a person's skin plays no part in love. Of what use will it be if you are married to a person from your own culture and yet live in an unhappy marriage where you are treated with no respect? However, we must thread very carefully when making the decision to marry someone who is not from our culture or from our country. The risk can be very high.

WHAT YOU DON'T KNOW ABOUT MARRIAGE

Before you make up your mind to marry, you must ask yourselves, this question: I am ready for marriage? Is the person I want to marry also ready for marriage? Why do I want to get married? Why do I want to be married to this particular person? Do I know him or her enough to be married to him or her? Do I really love him or I just like him or her? There is difference between loving someone passionately and liking someone. How truly are you convinced this is the person you want to spend the rest of your life with? How convinced I am that the person I am getting married to will live up to the marriage vows? Is there something about his or her life I need to know before we get married? Could you look into the future and say I am happy I am getting married to this person? Do you know that the most important thing about marriage is not present but the future?

Do I know much about his or her family? It is important couples planning to get married find enough information about the marital history of their spouse's family. Do not dismiss this advice. It can reveal much about the person you want to marry. It is very important you search the marital history of the family you are about to be married into, because it may tell you what to expect in the future when you are married.

There are some marital problems that run in some families from generation to generation that could either be spiritual or physical of which you may not know. For example, they may be a curse in the family which you may not know about. Family curses are responsible for so many marital problems. The problem with some of these family curses is that you may never know it is the cause for problem you are encountering in your marriage until it is too late. And before you realize the root cause of the problem much harm has been done already. Certain curses are irrevocable except through divine intervention.

The causes of so many marriage failures are buried deep in some families' history. If a man or woman marries into such a family he or she is bound to face marital problems. Where couples come from the same culture, it is very easy to detect marital problems that run in some families because some families do investigate families from which their son or daughter is going to marry.

The sad story of a young Christian woman in our church is a good illustration of how some curses can destroy some Christian marriages. Judith comes from a family of five girls and two boys; she is the youngest of the five sisters. When her elder sister got married and became pregnant the whole family were very happy and overjoyed. But the happiness soon turned into sorrow after the birth of her son. When the son was one year old, the husband divorced her sister without any reason. Then, one after the other all four remaining sisters got married and all faced the same fate as the elder sister. What the sisters did not know was that, there was a curse in the family against all the female children. As soon as each of the sisters got married and had a baby she was divorced by her husband without any good reason. When Judith married her childhood sweetheart she became very happy. When she became pregnant and gave birth to a beautiful baby girl, her husband who is a Christian started behaving very strangely towards her. The slightest thing she did irritates her husband who then overreacted negatively. Her loving husband suddenly became very temperamental and annoyed over issues that would normally not cause any problem in the family.

As a result of her husband's rather strange behaviour a group of us from the Church's intercession prayer team went to pray for her. But the fear of the curse in the family had overwhelmed her. Fear is a formidable weapon in the hands of the devil which he uses to reduce Christians from the status of mighty warriors to that of frightened schoolchildren. Instead of looking onto Jesus Christ, she was looking at the impending curse that was about to ravage her marriage.

Grandmother once told me that the more we fix our eyes on our problem, the more the problem becomes bigger and God becomes smaller. But if we fix our eyes on God during our troubled times, God becomes bigger and the problems become smaller. The fear of the curse paralyzed her faith in Jesus Christ. In her own words, she said, "Four of my senior sisters have all been divorced after giving birth to their first baby so what prevents me from going through the same fate?" When her daughter was five her husband moved out of the matrimonial home and married someone else. Of all the sisters, she was the only one whose marriage had survived beyond two years. If only she could have fixed her eyes on Jesus and the promises of God her marriage would have survived the storm of the curse. But the thought of the curse had such a profound effect on her marriage and spiritual life that she kept expecting the worst. What she did not know was that from the day she gave her life to Christ, the curse ceased to have an effect on her, which means the power of the curse on her had been broken through the cleansing blood of Jesus Christ. However, by resurrecting the curse through fear and the thought of how the curse had ravaged the marriages of her sisters, she easily succumbed to the power of the curse.

Certain marriages break down without any tangible reason while other marriages break down over issues that should not cause any problem. Sometimes a spouse will make a mountain out of a molehill for absolutely no reason. When you begin to see these signs in your marriage then know that they are an indication of spiritual problems. Except it be revealed to you, it will take the spirit of discernment to know the causes of the spiritual problems going on in your marriage. A spiritual problem in a marriage can easily be overcome by taking it to the taking it to the LORD in prayer. But remember, spiritual problems in marriage do not go away without fasting and prayers. It takes the following to win the spiritual battles in your marriage:

1. **The Word of God:** Our ability to tap into the unlimited resources of God's promises in the Bible and use this as a spiritual weapon. With the word of God we can draw on limitless power that can see us through trials and develop a sustaining vision that can help us tackle the spiritual problems in our marriage and keep us moving forward.

2. **Prayer:** Prayer destroys the Gospel's enemies and loose Satan and his grip on our marriage. Prayer, when used effectively, can loosen us from a curse that has bound us and caused problems in our marriage. With prayer we can capture the same powerful vision that kept Christians in the first century centred and focused on Christ. Even when they faced fearsome persecution at the hands of their enemies, they held on to their faith in Jesus Christ.

3. **Fasting:** The denial of physical needs such as food and water in order to feed ourselves spiritually holds the key to unlocking the door that will draw us close to God for the purpose of seeking the face of God in dealing with the issues in the marriage. Fasting empties the Christian of physical desires and physical weakness and instead fills us with spiritual desires and spiritual strength.

How sad, that most Christians do not study the Bible so they do not know the promises of God in order to enable them to tap into God's limitless resources. How can a Christian know the promises of God if he or she does not read and study the Scriptures? It is only by reading and studying the Scriptures that the Christian can experience change within. About seventy percent of Christian in every congregation do not read nor study the Scriptures. The only time they read or hear the word of God is from the pulpit. In some Churches, prayer meetings are always very well attended, but the Bible study classes are virtually empty. The question is: why?

The difference between Bible study and prayer meetings are:

1. **Prayer:** prayer meeting are battlegrounds where spiritual battles are fought.
2. **Bible Study:** Bible study classes are a training ground where Christians are trained in how to fight with weapons of spiritual warfare.
3. **Bible Study Classes:** are designed to make the Christian battle-ready.
4. **Bible Study Classes:** Christians are given training on the devices of the devil and how to

take a redemptive strike before the enemy takes you by surprise. A good General will not draft a soldier into a battlefield without adequately training and arming the soldier. A Christian who is not well equipped will be no match for Satan and his team of demonic forces. Christians must be battle ready before taking on the devil and his team of demonic forces.

A friend who is a retired Army Colonel and now a pastor of a church once said this about spiritual warfare, "Hard on the training ground and easy on the battlefield." What this implies is that, the Bible study classes are the training ground for spiritual battle. Christians who attend Bible classes and study the Scriptures at home are better equipped for spiritual battle. Christians who know and understand the Scriptures can take on the devil and his team of demonic forces and prevail. Spiritual battle is not for Christians who can only pray without being equipped with the Word of God; rather it is for Christians who study the Word of God, obey the Word of God and who can pray the prayer that sends shivers down the spines of the enemy.

The Devil and his team of demonic forces do not fear prayers, what they fear is the Word of God. The writer of Hebrews wrote the following, "For the word of God is living and active. Sharper than any double-edged sword, it penetrates even to dividing soul and spirit, joins and marrow; it judges the thoughts and attitudes of the heart. Nothing in all creation is hidden from God's sight. Everything is uncovered and laid bare before the eyes of him to whom we must give account" (Hebrews 4:12-13).

The moment a Christian starts praying, he or she is declaring war on the devil and the devil will not take it lightly. There is nothing that provokes the devil like a Christian praying. Do not wake a sleeping giant if you cannot take him on in a battle. The devil and his team of demonic forces are not mere feeble forces. It takes a Christian, who has,

1. Knowledge of the Word of God.
2. Belief the Word of God.
3. Understanding the promises of God.

Prayer is like an empty gun and the Word of God is the bullet. Combine these two and they become the most formidable weapon to root out the enemy's stronghold and expose their evil plots. These two weapons are the most feared weapons in Satan's kingdom; when used effectively they can rock the kingdom of darkness to its core.

Those planning to get married have to be very careful because deception runs deep in the heart of many people and this you will never know until after honeymoon is over. The essence of this book is to make young people aware of what they have not prepared for in cross-cultural marriage. For you to succeed in your marriage you have to work for it. A good and successful marriage does not come by without hard work and change of attitude. People in good and loving marriage worked hard for it. It is the way we see each other in our marriage that will determine if we can succeed.

Marriage can be likened to a child learning how to walk. When the child takes few steps and falls, then he or she tries falls again. The fall does not make the child stop making further attempt. The more the child falls, the more determined the child is to try again. The bruises a child suffers as a result of so many falls are only to remind the child of what to expect as he walks into adulthood.

Marriage is full of pitfalls; those who are not prepared before going into marriage will be faced with disappointment. It takes hard work and determination to succeed. Marriage is not for quitters and quitters do not succeed in their marriage. Grandmother once said, "We marry the person we love to work with him or her to make the marriage succeed no matter the storms that rise. "

In marriage, many people think more about the wedding and its preparations than what happens afterwards. Marriage is about how to live happily and enjoy life with person you are married to. Marriage is a long journey and only fittest and those who are determined to obey its rules and walk only with the person they started the journey with can complete it.

In another example, a Christian friend told me of a curse that nearly wiped out the female members of his family. This is how the story unfolds; his great grandmother gave birth to seven children. After the seventh child she became pregnant again and gave birth to twins. She died immediately after giving birth to the twin. His grandmother also had five children before giving birth to a set of twins. Three months after giving birth she died.

His mother gave birth to three girls and two boys. Soon after this she became pregnant and gave birth to twins boys. Then the bad omen that has ravaged the family resurfaced and killed the woman barely a week after giving birth to the twins.

Following this, two of his sisters died after giving birth to twins, then the younger sister, who was a Christian, married a Christian brother in a colourful weeding. Two years after her marriage she gave birth to her first son. Then she became pregnant again and gave birth to another son. Now the young family needed a baby girl to complete the family because they planned to have three children.

When she became pregnant with the third child the family were so excited and hoping for a baby girl. But little did they know their dream of a complete family was about to be shattered. When the babies were born the midwife told her she had beautiful twin girls. At this, she turned her face away from the children and started crying. This made the midwife ask her, "Why are you crying, are you not happy to have these twins?" When she did not answer, the mid-wife repeated the question. When the midwife saw that she did blink or move her body, she called for assistance. By the time the doctor on duty arrived, she was dead.

The mystery surrounding this whole saga was that the couple in question were committed Christians. One would have thought that the curse could not have an effect on the couple. A curse that runs in a family will have no spiritual or physical effect on a member of that family who becomes a Christian. The problem here is that when Christians sit down and do nothing about a spiritual problem that runs in the family just because they are Christians, they are likely to experience spiritual problems.

We need to ask the following questions.

1. Why did she cry when she could pray?
2. Where was her faith in Christ?
3. Did she not know about the curse?
4. Why did she not claim the promises of God?
5. Did she not believe in the power of prayer and the power of the living Word?
6. Why did she give in to the devil?

7. Why did she forget Jesus Christ is the answer to the curse?
8. Did her pastor know of the curse?
9. What did the church not intercede for the couple?
10. Where were the husband and the pastor during delivery?

Although a family may be bound by a curse, the curse itself becomes powerless in the life of a member of the family who becomes a Christian. There is not a family curse that cannot be broken or reversed. It takes the prayer of a spirit filled Christian to release a person under the spell of a curse. A curse has no hold on a praying Christian who lives his or her life in obedience to the Word of God.

The sad situation of the Christian family above raises many questions. It brings back sad memories of my aunt's children. She gave birth to seven boys. Two of them are doctors, one a lawyer; two of them are businessmen and one a politician. All seven of the children can only father children outside wedlock. The moment they are married they cannot have children. Those of them who married before having children are childless.

Why some Christians wait until they are overwhelmed with problems before running to God is baffling. The young lady and her fiancé knew of the curse in the family and should have done something about it during their courtship before they even got married. If their faith was rooted and grounded in Jesus Christ, the situation could have been different today. If they had sought spiritual help before they got married she would have been alive to tell the story of how God intervened and broke the power of a curse in her family.

The Oxford Advance Learner's Dictionary defines a curse as a word or phrase that has magical powers to make bad things happen; something that causes harm or evil. Anger and bitterness are the root causes that have resulted in a curse being pronounced on some families. When a person is consumed with bitterness because of what someone might have done to him or her can cause the person offended to pronounce a curse. Sometimes a family may not know they are under a curse until harm has been done. This is because the person or the family that pronounced the curse did it in secret without telling those it concerned.

Now let's turn our attention to the Scripture and see how curses created problems in the life of individuals and families.

1. The first people in the Bible to have been cursed were Adam and Eve. Now let's see what led to the Curse. In Scripture, a repeated warning is usually given before a curse is pronounced but with human curse a warning is seldom given. **Warning:** *And the LORD God commanded the man, "You are free to eat from any tree in the garden; but you must not eat from the tree of the knowledge of good and evil, for when you eat of it you will surely die."* We see clearly here that a warning was given and the consequence of the curse was irrevocable. Now the pronounced curse: *"Cursed is the ground because of you; through painful toil you will eat of all the days of your life. It will produce thorns and thistle for you and you will eat the plants of the field. By the sweat of your brow you will eat your food until you return to the ground, since from it you were*

taken; for dust you are and to dust you will return." Genesis 2:16-17 & Genesis 3:17:19

2. The second person we will turn our attention is Cain. **The warning:** *Then the LORD said to Cain, "Why are you angry? Why is your face downcast? If you do what is right, will you not be accepted? But if you do not do what is right, sin is crouching at your door; it desires to have you, but you must master it."* The LORD in His mercy reasoned with, Cain, giving him two alternatives: 1) If he did well, he would be accepted, and 2) If he did not do right, sin, like a ferocious beast, crouch at the door ready to spring on him and devour him. Cain paid no attention to the warning of the LORD. Instead of acknowledging his fault and making things right he nursed his wounded pride. As a result, his resentment grew and soon jealousy and envy turned into murderous hate. Then the terrible deed was done he murdered his brother. Now listen to the curse: The LORD said to Cain, "What have you done? Listen! Your brother's blood cries out to me from the ground. Now you are under a curse and driven from the ground, which open its mouth to receive your brother's blood from your hand. When you work the ground, it will no longer yield its crops for you. You will be a restless wanderer on the earth."

3. The first two curses above were pronounced by God on man because of disobedience. The third curse we will examine is the first curse pronounced by a human. The curse was as a result of anger and bitterness, which a father pronounced on his son. Let's see what happened that made Noah pronounce such a harsh curse on his son. Noah got himself so drunk that he went

to bed naked. His youngest son saw his nakedness, and instead of covering him, he told his elder brothers. The brother promptly reacted as the Scripture states, *"But Shem and Japheth took a garment and laid it across their shoulders; then they walked in backwards and covered their father's nakedness. Their faces were turned the other side so that they would not see their father's nakedness.* **Noah's reaction** was that of hurt, anger and bitterness. **Then he pronounced the curse:** *"Cursed be Canaan! The lowest of the slave will be to his brothers." He also said, "May Canaan be the slave of Shem."(Genesis* 9:20-27). The difference between curses pronounced by God and that pronounced by humans is that God warns us before a curse is pronounced. But with human curse is pronounced as a result of hurt, anger and bitterness. Therefore warnings are not given. Human curses are spontaneous. They curse before they even think of the consequences of their action. We can see this from the example of Noah's curse on his younger son. Noah's curse was born out of pure hurts which lead to anger and bitterness. The picture of Noah lying drunk in his tent is a shameful spectacle, but it contains moral significance. Surely he could not have been ignorant of the effect of wine. From this one would be tempted to ask this question: It is possible for a man to maintain a spotless life before a godless world and then fall into temptation in his home? Temptations from within a person are often more deadly than the ones from the outside. Long years of spiritual victory will not guarantee that we will always be free from sin. "So, if you think you are standing firm, be careful that you do not fall." (1 Corinthians 10:12)

4. Curses are the result of demeaning or painful situations that someone has put another person through causing bitterness and anger. To illustrate this, let's take the deception of the Gibeonite. This is what Joshua did when he discovered that he had been deceived: Then Joshua summoned the Gibeonite and said, "why did you deceive us by saying, 'we live a long way from you,' while actually you are near us? You are under a curse: You will never cease to serve as woodcutter and water-carriers for the house of God."

5. Another example of how someone can pronounce a curse because of a painful situation can be found in 2 Kings 2. 23-25. *From there Elisha went up to Bethel. As he was walking along the road, some youths came out of the town and jeered at him. "Go on up, you baldhead!" they said, "Go on up, you baldhead!" He turned around, looked at them and called down a curse on them in the name of the LORD. Then two bears came out of the woods and mauled forty-two of the youths.*

6. In another example, a man unlawfully seized a parcel of land from his childhood friend because of his wealth and influence. When his friend's wife became seriously sick he needed money for his wife's medical treatment so he approached his friend for a loan. To his surprise, his rich friend asked for collateral before the loan can be given. This poor man used a parcel of land which was his family inheritance as the collateral in order to save his wife. The using of the parcel of land as collateral meant this man had been

deprived of his only means of supporting his family, because he depended on the land for farming. After three years, the poor man was able to raise money to pay his friend. But to his surprise, when he went to pay the money, his friend told him, "Sorry: You are one month late in paying back the loan. I don't need the money any more, you keep it and I will keep the land as my property." As a result of this rich man's behaviour, the matter was taken to the town's local council for arbitration. But the rich man used his influence in the community to keep the parcel of land. The poor man begged his friend to return the family inheritance for his money but the rich man refused. The poor man walked out of the arbitration a broken man filled with bitterness, anger and resentment. He became a laughingstock in the community. In his bitterness, he pronounced the following curse on his friend, "Your only son will never hear the cry of a baby in his life and all male children both born and unborn in your family will never have children." When the rich man's son's wife became pregnant she died eight month into the pregnancy. He remarried and the second wife also became pregnant and died three month before the baby was due. By this time the rumours started spreading that there was a curse in the family or the young man was up to something sinister. He married the third time and his new wife became pregnant. Seven months into the pregnancy, she started bleeding heavily. A friend of the wife took her to see a pastor who prayed for her. It became clear through revelation that her husband's father had taken a parcel of land that belongs to someone, and unless his father returned that parcel of land and ask for forgiveness the curse will never be broken. The wife told her husband of the prophecy, who in turn confronted his father. The young man's father confessed of the evil he did to his own friend. Finding the man was now the problem for the rich man, his son and wife. Nevertheless, through the most marvellous work of God they were guided by a prophecy that took them to the town where the man now lived. The man was found seriously sick on his deathbed. When the son of the rich man saw him, he fell at his feet and begged for the sins of his father to be forgiven. He offered to restore back three times what his father had taken from him. Then the poor man sat upright and asked the young man to kneel before him. Then he stretched his right hand over the young man's head and said' "I revoke the curse I pronounced on your father and his children. You are hereby set free from the curse. Rise up and go in peace." Then the rich man and his son hugged the man thanking him for setting the family free from the curse, but the man they hugged was a dead man. The man died as soon as he had broken the curse. The dreadful thing about curses is that in many cases the person who caused the problem that led to the pronouncing of the curse sometimes escapes the full effect of the curse. In most cases it is the innocent members of the family who suffer the effect of the curse.

From the various examples above we can see what causes some people to pronounce curses on those who put them through demeaning situations. Certain actions can provoke others to pronounce a curse. Sometimes, simple things like hurtful gossip can cause someone to pronounce a curse that can affect an entire generation.

Betrothal: An agreement to marry. This system of marriage can turn sinister where the family of the girl takes money from a man promising to give their daughter's hand in marriage when she is of age. There are cases where two families because of business association promise to have their son to marry their business partner's daughter. This can take place where the children involved are very young to know any thing about marriage. Some betrothal can take place at birth.

There are instances where even older men marry girls young enough to be their daughters or grand children. This reminds me of Elizabeth a class-mate of mind in high school. At the age of six she was betrothed to a business man who was her father's friend. When her father's business run into financial difficulties, creditors threatened to confiscate and sell off his entire assets.

Against this, he asked for help from his friend who happened to be a distance family. The man agreed to give him twice the money he needed on condition that he willow him to marry his daughter when she is eighteen. Elizabeth's father willing agreed to the man's terms. The man asked Elizabeth's father to arrange a meeting between him and the elders of both families so that the agreement could be signed with the families as witnesses.

Elizabeth was a beautiful mixed race girl, who grew to become a very beautiful and intelligent woman who wanted a career in medicine. But the man she was betrothed to was by now old enough to be her grandfather stood in her way to become a doctor. When Elizabeth gain admission into university to read medicine this man appeared from obscurity and demanded to marry his betrothed wife.

When Elizabeth's family told the man they were willing to pay back his money with interest he refused and held the agreement in his hand and said; "I stand by this agreement and there is nothing to be contested in the agreement. You must allow me to marry Elizabeth." When the rich man realised the family were becoming difficult he warned Elizabeth's family he will use every means to get what lawfully belongs to him by virtue of the agreement signed.

When Elizabeth's family realised that the rich man was up to something sinister they gave in to his demand and forced their daughter to marry the rich man. The rich man loved Elizabeth so much that after their wedding he handed his entire business empire for Elizabeth to manage. Within four years after their marriage her husband died of natural causes leaving her with two children.

A STEP INTO MARRIAGE

For the Christian choosing a life partner for the first time is a serious matter that requires the direction of the LORD. This is true because "a prudent wife is from the LORD." (Proverb 19:14). A wise Jewish king once wrote this statement: A wife of a noble character who can find? She is worth far more than rubies. Her husband has full confidence in her and lacks nothing of value" (Proverbs 31:10-12).

A step into marriage involves so many factors that a person looking to get married should consider, but all of them cannot be discussed in this book. Also since customs differ so greatly from one culture to another, it is difficult to generalize to any degree on the subject. It is possible, however, to state some general principles that can prove helpful either to one who is seeking a husband or wife or to those who are in the process of working toward marriage.

In some cultures, the influence of parents and friends may be the main consideration in a young man's choice of life partner. In others, people order than the young man and young woman who are to be married make the decision. Whatever the selection process, rarely does one person have all the qualities that make a good marriage partner. This is one reason why the choice is not easy no matter who makes it. The choice of a life partner must be made with ones life, calling, and ultimate goals in view. This requires time, patience, careful consideration and above all, fasting and prayer.

While it is better to know what God's will is before one makes such a decision, this is not always possible.

In some cases one will have married already and established a home before he or she finds Jesus Christ as Saviour and LORD. In these situations, one obviously neither knew about nor considered Biblical principles when he or she made the choice. As we shall see, knowing what the Bible says about the respective roles of each marriage partner is crucial to one's success in marriage.

Let's look at two verses that show us the importance of marriage from God's viewpoint. At a very early point in man's existence, God said, "It is not good for man to be alone, I will make a helper suitable for him" (Genesis 2:18). Much more later, Jesus, looking back to the origin of marriage, said "the Creator 'made them male and female,' and said, 'For this reason a man will leave his father and mother and be united to his wife, and the two will become one flesh.' So they are no longer two, but one" (Matthew 19:4-6). God ordained marriage to provide mutual support, companionship and unity. Thus marriage is important because it meets these psychological and physical needs. A good marriage is important for everyone, but it is even more important for the Christian.

The Roles within Marriage: Whether you are already married or planning to get married, it is extremely important to understand the respective Biblical roles of the husband and wife and their relationship with each other and with their children. Understanding these concepts is one of the most important factors in making an intelligent selection of a life partner. Furthermore, it helps a new husband and wife establish and maintain a harmonious relationship, and it enables each to understand the needs and legitimate expectations of the other.

The Concept of Role: The term role refers to the behaviour expected from a person who occupies a given position or status. In one society, for instance, the husband is expected to play a certain role, which may be different from the role of the husband in another culture. The husband begins to learn about various roles as a child in the home, and he learns more about them as he comes into contact with other socializing agencies such as the church, school, and friends. By the time he approaches marriage, he has received socialization different from that of every other person. The same can be said for every other person who prepares for marriage; so each one has a different concept of the roles that he or she is expected to properly play as a husband or wife.

As a couple approaches marriage, one partner may be in conflict with the general cultural concept. Not infrequently, the roles of each conflict with those the Scripture describes. This problem is often made worse by different movements that arise from time to time. Some of these focus on radical changes that contradict traditional values. When this occurs and one is led to question what position to take, he may be assured that the Scriptures provide an objective, trans-cultural guide to appropriate family roles.

Biblical Role Concepts: The major passages in the New Testament concerning the roles of marriage and family are Ephesians 5:21-33, Colossians 3:18-20 and 1 Peter 3:1-7. In these Scriptural passages that deal with personal relationships, the writer begins with what is basic for the home, the relationship between husband and wife. It is significant that in these passages husbands and wives are reminded of their *duties to one another, rather than their rights.* In fact, the theme of *self-sacrifice* is significant throughout. "Submit to one

71

another out of reverence for Christ;" this theme is prominent in all the Bible teaching related to Christian love.

In Ephesians 5:21-33 in the discussion of husband-wife relationships, the first to be addressed is the role of the wife. A wife's duty is to submit herself to her "husband as to the LORD" (v.22), which indicates that she is submitting to the Lordship of Christ. While the New Testament emphasizes that men and women have spiritual equality before God (Galatians 3:28), nevertheless, for order and unity in the family, the responsibility for leadership and authority rests with the husband. With this responsibility, the duty of the husband is summed up in the word love. Love, as it is used in Ephesians 5:25 and the verse following, is the verb that corresponds to the noun love used in 1 Corinthians 13. This word signifies a self-denying, constant concern for the highest good of the other person. It is not only a practical concern for the other person's welfare but also a continual readiness to deny one's own pleasure for the help and benefit of the other.

Think of how *love* is described in 1 Corinthians 13. It is a love that is patient, kind, humble, courteous, trusting and supporting. It is love that makes one eager to understand the needs and interests of the other, and it does all it can to supply those needs. This is the type of *love* with which the husband should love his wife. He is to love his wife as "Christ also love the Church" (Ephesians 5:25), loving her as he does his own body (v.28). He is to show the same selfish concern for her welfare that he shows his own body. He is to have the same self-sacrificing love for his wife that Christ has for His bride, the church.

Marriage is an interdependent relationship with two branches. The husband represents one branch of that relationship and the wife the other. The husband may depend on the wife to help hold the marriage together and the wife also depend on the husband to keep the marriage together. Both branches depend on each other for the emotional and financial support. If either of the branches lets go, the relationship collapse.

In marriage the quest for independence can become a preoccupation and this can cause one of the branches to give way and fall off. Furthermore, the desire for one of the branches to stand alone and cast his or her shadow could lead to competition in the marital relationship. In the marital relationship both husband and wife must show strong identity with feelings of self-sufficiency. But above all a strong feeling of love must bind and hold both branches together.

Independency represents the ability to maintain one's own identity while sharing resources and values with a spouse in a compatible, intimate relationship. In marriage, each spouse must have a strong individual identity and relate meaningfully to each other. Remember, in marriage both branches are equal and neither one is above the other.

Eve's judgment in Genesis 3:16 have come under intense scrutiny from many interpreters, with widely divergent results. Modern feminism has motivated Christians to reconsider the role of women in the home, church, and society. The church has debated this verse vigorously in recent years because of its important implications.

Eve, as a representative of all women, received a twofold punishment in Genesis 3:16.

1. I will greatly increase your pains in childbearing; with pain you will give birth to children.
2. Your desire will be for your husband, and he will rule over you.

First, Eve will experience painful labour in childbirth. The very point at which she received her greatest sense of fulfilment in life, according to the Old Testament conventions, will also be a point of suffering. But in punishment also has a positive side, since it will be through her pain and childbirth that God will provide salvation for the world (3:15).

Second, Eve's relationship with her husband will be marred because of sin. Some have taken this verse to be **prescriptive,** or pronouncing a divine decree that women should or must remain submissive to their husbands. But this is an unfortunate misunderstanding of the words used in the verse.

The terms "desire" and "rule" in 3:16b are found again in 4:7b. Sin is like an animal that "desires to control and dominate Cain, but God challenged Cain to "rule" the unrestrained desire of sin. If, as seems likely, the author of Genesis intends us to read these verses together, the desires of Eve for her husband correspond to sin's desire to pounce on Cain. It is a desire to break the relationship of equality established at creation and transform it into a relationship of domination and servitude. "To love and to cherish" has degenerated into; "to desire and to dominate" (19).

We must not read Genesis 3:16b as God's decree for women to be subservient to men any more than we would take 3:16a as God's will for women to suffer as much pain as possible in childbirth. In other words, this passage is not **prescriptive,** but **descriptive.** It explains why women have pain in childbirth and how marriage, this most beautiful of human relationships, also holds potential for great abuse. But it in no way should be used to justify male tyranny in marriage. (Bill T. Arnold).

In his book *Introduction to Psychology: A Christian Perspective.* Raymond T. Brock states the following in

74

Steps to consider before marriage: *Goals to achieve;* Make a list of what you would like to accomplish in life. Establish specific goals one year and ten years from now.

Examination of information: How many of these goals are possible as a single? Make a list. How many require married? Make a list.

Information search: What additional information do you need to assist you in making a valid decision? Where can you secure the needed information, guidance or counsel?

Assessment of risk: How would being single assist or interfere with any of your goals? What would your goals in marriage delay?

Plan of action: Glean from your list what you consider the core values you must achieve to be a fulfilled person. Put an asterisk in front of those things that should be accomplished before marriage. Are you willing to delay marriage to achieve those goals? If not, are those goals really that important to you? What strain would it put on your marriage if you tried to reach those goals as a married person? What pressure would it put on a spouse or children if you tried to reach those goals after you started your family?

Decisions to be implemented: What should you do? Remain single? Plan for marriage? What goals would marriage delay? What goals would marriage hamper or eliminate?

Hopefully, by the time you have come to see that the decision to marry or remain single is not something to be determined while huddled in romantic seclusion. This decision is far too important to allow it to be influenced by chemistry or the moon's reflection on a romantic river. This approach to decision-making will not select the right person for you, but it will give you information about yourself that you need before you get your priorities straight and decide what the most important things in your life are.

As a final exercise, explore your romantic potential by responding to the following:

1. List five healthy reasons for remaining single.
2. List five unhealthy reasons for remaining single.
3. List five healthy reasons for getting married.
4. List five unhealthy reasons for getting married.
5. List some possible benefits for remaining single.
6. List some possible limitations of married life.
7. List some possible benefits of married life.
8. List some possible limitations of remaining single.

Some people don't really give a second thought before getting into a marital relationship while others don't have the slightest idea what marriage is all about. Their main concern is, "I am getting old and I should get married quickly before age catches up with me." Therefore, anyone that shows interest becomes my wife or husband without checking the person's background or who the person really is. It is far better to stay single than to be married to the wrong person.

Men and women preparing to go into marriage can be categorized into three main groups. We will begin with the following ages, between 19 to 24 years. Most women in this group think more about enjoying life rather than marriage. Marriage is not something they give immediate attention to for the following reasons.

1. **Education:** Most women in this group are more dedicated to their education. Therefore, they decide to spend much time in school to acquire a higher educational qualification. Sometimes

education becomes a barrier to marriage. A woman who is determined to succeed may have less time for marriage, and may see marriage as a stumbling block to success.

2. **Career success:** Is ambition wrong? Is it wrong to be driven for best? The difference between right and wrong ambition is in our goal and motivation whether it's for God's glory or self. Ambition oriented toward a happy and successful marriage is never focused on self. In a time when women are finding new opportunities, those who are determined to rise to the highest pinnacle of their career may put off marriage.

3. **Beginners:** Women in this group see themselves as women whose careers are about to begin and don't want marriage to distract them. They see marriage as a stumbling block to success in career. They build a life around success. Since age is on their side they become focused on their life ambition rather marriage and may resist any external pressure towards marriage.

4. **Youthfulness:** Their youthfulness is their trump card so they can afford to enjoy the best of life until they are ready to marry. Some women in this age group do not really think about marriage, and even when they do, they do not take marriage very seriously.

5. **Indulgences:** Some women's desire for luxury and pleasure goes beyond the extreme and may affect them later in life when they want to settle down to for a marital life. Some of them change partners like trading in used cars without any guarantee. While others sieve men like wheat.

Men above this age group who are serious about marriage should look beyond women in this group. The truth is that some women in this group are not ready for marriage. A young man looking to settle down will be wasting his time looking for a bride from this pasture. Women in this group do not want to miss out in life by being tied down with marriage. The idea of sampling sexual partners before marriage is like a deadly virus that will one day come to haunt them.

Some of the women in this group who get married are likely to get out quickly when things are not going as they had expected. Hence the high divorce rate among these group. Marriage is for the mature and strong-hearted and not for the immature and faint-hearted people. Marriage works only for those who understand what it means to be married and what to expect in marriage.

Some women in this group use marriage as a means of getting away from home, only to find out that what they were running away from is what will confront them in the marriage. Then, when they find out that they cannot cope with married life they feel trapped in an institution that sets a code of conduct for those who take its vows. The marriage institution is not about dos and don'ts, it is an institution that seeks to establish good moral conduct between husband and wife. Marriage is not about what your rights are but what your duty is.

Women in the red zone are more likely to try to continue their single life into the marital life. This is where the problem starts. The moment we enter the institution of marriage there is no turning back to the life we lived before. The person we are married to becomes the most important person to us and we build our life with him or her.

Finally, some of the women in this group are very dedicated to their marriage and are trustworthy when they settle down as married women. They easily adjust and blend into married life which allows them to put life outside the institution of marriage behind them, and move forward without looking back. There are countless women in the red zone who have been able to hold their marriage together because of their desire to make it work.

The second group of women that fall into what I call the green light zone or the ideal zone. They are women between the ages of 25 and 35 years. Women in this age group are ready for marriage and take relationship very seriously. Men looking for women for serious relationships will find women in this group ideal because women in this group are looking for relationships with commitment. The *green light* group of women are more interested in men who are serious about settling down for marriage rather than men who do not want commitment. Women in the *green* light age group are spiritually and physically mature. Women in this group are ideal women for any man looking for a wife. Usually women in the *ideal* group are looking for a serious relationship which can eventually be lead to marriage. They are known to avoid men who do not want commitment. Women in the ideal group will do anything to prevent age relegating them to the *desperate* age zone which is also called the *amber* age zone. Their mind and souls are prepared for marriage and nothing will distract them from joining the marriage institution.

Before we examine the third group we will look at three things that affect the third group, which are 1 *Family Pressure 2 Education and 3 Child Bearing.* The third group of women are what is called the *Amber group or the desperate* age group which ranges between the ages of 36 to 46. Women in this group are very vulnerable and subject to deception. Dishonest men prey on women in this group with the promise of marriage and then disappoint them after they have had enough of them.

Family Pressures: Most women in this group are very alert and cautious about men who show interest in them in order to avoid men who are not interested in commitment. Because of family pressure some are not able to discern the genuineness and the deceptive schemes of some men who have selfish motive and are only interested in relationships without commitment. Men who are only interested in relationships without commitment must be avoided. Women with pride and dignity should avoid sloppy Joes that are only after a jolly ride without commitment.

Some women in this group come under enormous pressure to get married. This is where the problem comes from, in desperation some walk blindly into marital unhappiness. Family pressure is a pitfall that has tricked so many women in this group into unhappy marriages. Men who don't want commitment in a relationship should be avoided by women who are looking for a relationship that will lead to marriage.

Education and Career Prospects: Is one of the major reasons why some women put off marriage till later in life. Women these days want to be well-educated before they even think of marriage which is a good thing. They may also aspire to get to the top managerial position or become head of a corporation and so defer marriage until later in life. The drive to succeed in life is the reasons why some women spend years in education to compete with their male counterparts for top corporate positions. Knowledge is power. But for women it comes with a price. That price is missing out on marriage and child-bearing. While it is good to aspire to the highest pinnacle of your profession, you have to be mindful of age if you desire to settle down as a married woman.

In most cases before they realise what is happening age has caught up with them. In their desperation, they commit a catalogue of errors. Women in this group become selective in the choice of prospective suitors. They base their criteria on a man's educational background and career success. Some women will not marry a man of a lower rank.

Child Bearing: Women who want children in marriage become desperate to marry and start a family. This then becomes their blind spot. Desperation is a breeding ground that attracts deceptive men who are only interested in a relationship without commitment. Women in this group are well advised to be on the look-out for men like this.

The good news is that women in the *amber group* make very good wives. Not only that, they are the *pearl of the marriage institution.* They know and understand what marriage is, and are never the trouble-makers in marriage. Women in this group guard and protect their marriage with their heart.

The other two groups we have not mentioned are what we call pleasure groups which are girls between the ages of 16 to 18 years. Men who are seriously thinking of settling down to a quiet married life should avoid these groups. Girls in this group are nothing but children who should be under the control of their parents. Girls in this group are not "ideal material for marriage." Girls in this group should be in college studying for a trade or for a higher qualification that will prepare them for the future, rather than thinking about marriage.

Marriage was never designed for children; therefore they should stay away from marriage. This does not mean children at this age cannot marry and have children because children at the tender age of 13 and 14 are known to have been married to men old enough to be their father or grandfather.

In some cultures it is normal for older men to take under age-children as wives as custom demands. Such marriages are not based on love; rather they are based on family interest which helps to seal two families' ties. Love in this kind of arranged marriage is supposed to develop as the couple live together.

The other group of pleasure women are those in the age group between 47 and 54 years. Is there hope for women in this group? Yes there is still hope for women in this group. There are some men who will take a bride from this group than go for a bride from the group discussed above. Women on this group are very submissive and loyal to their spouse.

I know of a Christian sister who married at the age of 49 and had three wonderful children for her husband. Today she is still happily married to her husband who is nine years younger than her. Although, older than her husband she is very submissive and addresses her husband as my Lord. The husband once said this about his wife; "I am glad I am married to Henrietta and no other woman."

Men: We will turn our attention to men and group them according to attitude towards marriage. The first group are known as the:

1. **Wavering group:** There are between the ages of 20 to 29. Some men in this group want to be in a relationship without commitment. Women who are serious about marriage should avoid this group completely. A woman looking for a relationship with commitment to marriage is well

advised to walk away from such men. Of what use will it be to waste your time in a relationship with a man who is only interested in companionship without any commitment? Some men in this group are never serious about marriage or prepared for marriage. People in this group can also be referred as the *cohabitation age.* Cohabitation usually begins at this age. They want to be in a relationship without any attachments. The fact is that they are simply not ready for marriage and a woman looking for a relationship with commitment will be wasting her time cohabiting with a man from this group. Some men in this group are like a quality control officer sitting at the end of production line sampling finished products. Some men at this age are known to change sexual partner just like trading in used cars. They cannot be trusted in any meaningful relationship. They are *free-floating* and as such are not looking for lasting relationships. All they want in a relationship is temporary pleasure and nothing else. Even when some men in this group get married, they can be very unstable in the relationship. While some of them are usually in and out of relationships, others become unsure whether they have made the right decision.

2. **The second group:** The second group of men we will look at are classified as the s*table men.* Their age ranges between 30 to 35 years. Men in these groups are very serious and are looking for stable relationships that will eventually lead to marriage. Men at this stage have accomplished much in the form of education and in their career. Therefore they want to crown their success by settling down as married men.

3. **The third group:** The third group of men are those whose age ranges between 36 to 45 years are what are referred to as the *Super Stable*. Most men at this stage are seriously looking forward to settling down in a happy marriage. Women who are looking for a peaceful marriage are better off seeking a bridegroom from this pasture. Most men from this group are loving and caring and would do anything to make the marriage a happy one.

4. **Late-comers:** They range between the ages of 46 to 55 Years. For men to wait until this age raise more questions. The reasons could be many. There are some men who have made up their mind never to marry, but later in life decides otherwise because of the fear of loneliness. Then they decide to marry but their marriage is mainly for companionship rather than the fulfilment of marriage as ordained by God. Some men who marry at this age usually don't want children because their desire to marry is purely based on companionship.

Timing is everything: Perfect timing is rare when it comes to looking for a man or woman you want to spend the rest of your life with. Nevertheless, God has a specific purpose and plan for His children who are looking to settle down as married spouses. Remember, God's timing is always perfect for those who are willing to wait on Him.

If you meet a man or woman who expresses interest in you, how would you know he or she is God's choice for you? Before we answer this question, let's turn our attention to three characters in the Bible that will help to deal with issues concerning our choice of future spouse and how to know the person we have set your heart on is the right person.

1. **Eliezer:** Abraham's chief servant. He put God to the test when he prayed the following prayer, "O LORD, God of my master Abraham, give me success today, and show kindness to my master Abraham. See, I am standing beside this spring, and the daughters of the townspeople are coming out to draw water. May it be that when I say to a girl, 'Please let down your jar that I may have a drink,' and she says, 'Drink, and I will water your camels too' Let her be the one you have chosen for your servant Isaac. By this I will know that you have shown kindness to my master." This man did what God absolutely requires of His children. **"Ask, Seek and Knock."** This man knew that God was the one who created the institution of marriage therefore He is the only one who is good enough to choose the right husband or wife for His children. The servant did not just go there and look at the girls and then choose the most beautiful girl among the maidens. True character is something which is obscure to man because no human can perceive what another is like. Dependency on God alone is the only way of avoiding being married to the wrong person. This Abraham's servant knew. He knew Isaac was a covenant child and had to be married to woman who fitted into that covenant. If a Christian knows who he or she is in Christ they would seek a wife or husband who fits perfectly into the covenant relationship they have with Christ. The servant went with an open mind, without a preconceived idea of the kind of maiden he was going to get

for Isaac, except that the maiden must come from Abraham's home town. This was all that he was equipped with. The rest was for God to choose. The servant's part in the mission was to go to Abraham's home town to look for the maiden. God's part in the mission was to choose the maiden. Choosing the maiden was not the servant's business but God's business. As Christians we must avoid playing the role of God. The warning here is that the moment we step out of God's plan, and then we are on our own. The prayers of Abraham's servant should serve as a guideline in allowing God to choose our future spouse. A Christian who is led by the Spirit will yield to the Spirit of God. In the days of Abraham, the Spirit of God was not permanently resident in the life of the people of God as we are fortunate to have the Holy Spirit dwelling in us. Yet they walked with God and totally depended on Him in their day to-day-life. Today, Christians who claim to have the Holy Spirit allow themselves to override what is God's choice for them.

2. **Samson:** The second character we will examine. In contrast to Abraham's servant prayer by asking God for a sign. Samson on other hand did not seek the face of God concerning the woman he wanted as a wife. In his quest to marry a woman of his choice against the wish of his parents he allowed his feelings towards the woman to override the godly advice of his parents. Now let's listen to what happened; "Samson went down to Timnah and saw there a young Philistine woman. When he returned, he said to his father and mother, "I have seen a Philistine woman in Timnah; now get her for me

as my wife." His father and mother replied, "Isn't there an acceptable woman among your relatives or among all our people? Must you go to the uncircumcised Philistine to get a wife? But Samson said to his father, "Get her for me. She's the right one for me" (Judges 14:1-3).

3. **Rebekah:** Is the third character we will examine. The scripture tells us that when Rebekah became pregnant, the babies jostled each other within her, and she said, "Why is this thing happening to me? So she went to enquire of the LORD." Our ability to know that there is something spiritually wrong with us holds the key to unlock our problems. When the babies started jostling each other, Rebecca knew what was going on was unnatural so she had to find answers to the problem, and her prompt search yielded results. If Rebecca had done nothing about the unusual movement of the unborn babies in her womb she would never have known the cause of the problem. She would have sat down brooding over a problem that could lead to stress. For example, if you are praying for a husband or a wife and someone prophesises that this man is your future husband, what criteria can you use to cross-examine if the prophesy is divine or false? Should we just believe any prophesies because they came from a pastor, a prophetess, a prophet, an elder or a Deacon? The fact that a prophecy is coming from the mouth of a Christian does not mean that the prophecy is divine. Only Christians who don't study the Scriptures are fooled by prophecy. The reason we marry is to fulfil God's divine plan for marriage. God's divine plan for marriage is for the family to be a channel of worship and fellowship with Him. But when

marriage breaks down, it brings shame to members of God's family.

4. **Gideon:** Is the fourth person in the Bible we will talk about. Now let's listen to the dialogue with the angel of the LORD. "If now, I have found favour in your eyes, give me a sign that it is really you talking to me." You can read the rest of the story for yourself. The key words in the dialogue are the words 'Give me a sign.' As a Christian praying for a husband or wife if you meet someone that fits all the criteria you want in a man or woman, how can you prove that the woman or man you have chosen is His choice for you? Before the angel of the LORD'S visitation Gideon was not filled with Holy Spirit; the reason is before Christ, the spirit of God was not permanently resident in His people.

5. It was only when God wants to use an individual that the Holy Spirit comes upon that person. Besides, all Gideon knew about God was from what his parent told him and the history of his people; beyond that he knew nothing of the Spirit of God. Based on the information he knew about God he acted promptly by the desire to know from the God of his ancestors if it was Him really talking to him. We see at this stage that Gideon needed confirmation. He did not act on the basis of what the angel told him, rather he wanted to be sure of the words of the angel when he said, "I will be with you, and you will strike down all the Midianites together." We see from the Scriptures that Gideon carried out a series of test to be sure he would not be going into a battlefield without God on his side.

Many Christian do not have the patience of Gideon to cross-examine the voices they are hearing because they are interested in what they are hearing. When person is interested in a prophetic message that has something to do with his or her future he has no time to check if the message is divinely inspired or is inspired by a false spirit. You meet a man or woman who expresses interest in you and you hear conflicting voices telling you this is the man or girl God has chosen for you. What would you do? Is this what you will do in such circumstances?

1. **Education:** First they will look at the man's educational background, and then find out what he studied. A young woman once said, "It is what a person studies at university that counts and not that he has degree from university."

2. **Social standing:** Some will find out what the man does for a living which is a good thing, but to find out what role or position he has in the company raises questions about your intentions and the type of men some women are looking for.

3. **Physical appearance:** Some women already know the kind of men they are looking for when it comes to the physical structure of men. Physical appearance is good but can be very deceptive. The physical appearance of a man does not mean everything about the man is complete. Some physically good looking men could have some handicap in other areas of the life a woman would not know until after the honeymoon. Never marry a man because of his good looks.

4. **Wealth:** What happens when the music stops? Wealth is known to be the blind spot of most

women. Most women think money can bring peace of mind in marriage while others think money brings joy in marriage. To marry a man because of his wealth comes with its problems. For an example, let's use the story of Nancy as a good illustration. Nancy and her three siblings were raised alone when their father died while they were all in their teens. She became a Christian at the age of fifteen. Ten years later she was married to s very rich and good-looking man. She met the man in their church. When the man first approached her she turned the man down because he was much older than she. While she was twenty-five he was forty. The man was so in love with Nancy that he started visiting Nancy's mother and showering her with money and expensive gifts. Nancy's mother was overwhelmed with the angelic appearance of the man, his wealth and good looks. She told her daughter; "It is this man or no man." Despite the pressure from her mother, an inner voice told her not to marry the man. Each time the mother brought up the issue of the marriage, an inner voice kept telling her, "This man is not the right man for you." She consulted her pastor for advice. This is what he told her, "I know Deacon Edwards to be a very good Christian for the past ten years. During this period there has not been any bad report about him both in the Church and outside of it. Everyone in the Church can testify this about him. I think this is the man God has chosen for you. And I prophesise that, three years from this day, the first day of May you and your husband will be blessed with a baby son." Even while the prophecy was going on, the inner voice kept telling her the man was not the husband for her. When she got home her mother confronted her with the following words, "Look, my daughter, I cannot lead you astray, I am your mother and I cannot give you bad advice. I am old enough to tell you what is good for you. I am after your future security, happiness and the joy of your marriage. Please, my daughter, if you respect me as a mother who bore you in my womb and gave birth to you then you, must trust my judgment and marry this man." Nancy accepted the man's proposal and married the man in a lavish wedding that became the talk of the town. For the six year of marriage they had sex six times which means they had sex once a year. The husband had an erection once a year. And even with that erection, sex was nothing but rape. The husband simply jumped on her and in a matter of seconds it was over. Then, the husband would be gasping for breath as if he had just finished a marathon race. After this, Nancy would have to wait another year for the husband to have an erection. Because of the bedroom problem, Nancy suggested they seek medical advice from specialist. This the husband agreed to but when the appointment came he had an excuse not to attend. When Nancy realised that her husband was up to something best known to him alone she spoke to her mother after two years. This is what the mother told her, "Have patience with your husband for him to sort out his sex life and things will soon be fine." When the bedroom problems did not improve, Nancy went back the second time for advice. She told her mother, "I desperately need children." In reply, her mother told her, "Why don't you sleep with your brother-in-law to have children for your husband?" At this, Nancy told her, "Sorry mum I cannot do what you are asking me to do because it will be a sin against God and unfaithfulness to my husband." Nancy went home and confided in her husband the demeaning suggestion. Surprisingly her husband told her, "If you think this would be good for us, then go ahead with it." She told her husband, "Sorry, I cannot do it." Nevertheless, in her desperation to have children she had to engage the services of a young man she knows very well during college through whom she became pregnant. The pregnancy turned her husband against her. He resented and called her all sorts of names. When she could no longer bear the humiliation from her husband, she went to speak to their pastor. This is what her pastor told her, "I don't believe what you are telling me. What interests me is that I prophesised you would become pregnant and have a baby. Calculating from the date of your pregnancy, it will coincide with the prophecy date." The pastor was only interested in the fulfilment of the prophecy and not the plight of a tormented married woman. When Nancy realised that the three people who tricked her into an unhappy marriage were each not interested in her problems but their own interest, she walked out of the marriage before death knocked on her door. A mother driven by greed, a pastor driven by pride of his prophecy being fulfilled and a husband who became a celibate except for once every year, all formed part of the link that drove this young woman to where she now finds herself. The question is: which of these three have destroyed the life of this young woman? Certain cultures allows parents to have so much influence over their children when it comes to marriage that the children simply don't have any choice but to go along with their parent's decisions. The Hebrew word for still means "to cease striving." It is the concept of putting your hands down and letting God intervene in your situation without your interference. This word picture is very interesting since we often use our hands in pushing things out of our way, to protect ourselves or strike back. When we drop our hands, it makes us feel defenceless and vulnerable. If Nancy had not interfered with her marital problems and allowed God to deal with the problem she would have been still married to her husband. To begin with, God gave her warnings about the impending marriage by means of doubt and inner feelings about being married to that man. Instead of taking the inner voice seriously as a warning from God about her fiancé, she blindly listened to her mother and is now reaping the consequences of her disobedience. On the other hand, she could have taken it to God in prayer; this too she failed to do and instead put her faith in her pastor. When we put our faith in men who are mere mortals subject to mistakes, we reap the evil of disobedience. A marital problem requires the Christian to run to God and not humans who are in most cases bound to lead us astray. For the Christian, allowing God to intervene in our problems is the best way for a trouble-free marriage.

For example, after spending years praying for a husband or wife, someone in your Church or outside the Church expresses interest in you. On what basis can you make up your mind if he or she is God's choice for you? Remember, marriage has to do with choosing one person out of all the people who approach you wanting to spend the rest of their life with you. Some people channel their affection through feeling rather than love. However, feeling has nothing to do with love. Feeling can be defined as a person's emotions rather than their thoughts. The feelings a man has towards a woman cannot be regarded as love because feelings do not seek the person's highest interest. Expression of emotional or sexual feelings toward a person is not the same as love.

Example Two: As a young man or woman you are faced with a lot of people expressing interest in you with the desire to marry you. How do you sieve through the chaff and separate the wheat. Situations like these create a breeding ground for deception. Women are more vulnerable in these kinds of situations than men. It very difficult to know and understand what goes on in the minds of some people when it comes looking for a bride or a bridegroom.

When it comes to marriage, most people have made up their mind as to the kind of man or woman they want to marry. The problem here is that the moment we make up our mind about the kind of husband or wife we are looking for, we may end up shutting God out of our search for our spouse. When a person's heart is fixed on something he or she desire they forget about God. They only run back to God when the desire turns bitter in their mouth.

The writer of Hebrews wrote the following words to his Jewish audience. They are worth reading because; through them we can learn to depend on God, who alone knows the future. "Nothing in all creation is hidden from God's sight. Everything is uncovered and laid bare before the eyes of him to whom we must give account" (Hebrews 4:13).

Have you been disappointed by someone you love and wanted to marry when at the last moment, he or she said "sorry I don't think we are compatible." To illustrate this clearly I use the example of a Christian sister in our church who is a solo gospel musician. When she was engaged to one of the elders in the Church, we were all happy for them. We kept praying for them until a young pastor was transferred to the Church.

The arrival of the pastor stalled the relationship between the sister and the Elder. As a result, she kept putting back the date of the wedding. A year after the pastor arrived, the sister made the following statement, "I am fully persuaded that my engagement to brother "B" was a mistake and I am now fully convinced marrying him is not the will of God, although we both love each other" (name withheld).

Distraught and unable to speak about the separation the brother walked away into a life of seclusion. Nine months after this separation the pastor married the sister in a colourful wedding. After the marriage, the assistant pastor was promoted and posted to a new station. Grandmother once said, "The reason we marry is the very reason that will take us down the road of divorce."

What this sister thought was a marriage made in heaven turn out to be a marriage made in hell. The Scriptures exposes the devil in three areas: 1 **he is a thief whose job is to steal 2; his desire is to kill and 3; he wishes to destroy our happy relationship with Christ.** The warning here is that those who fall in love with the devil do so because they refuse to believe what the Scripture is saying about the devil. Those who sit in the Church and take a bride or bridegroom from the devil will surely have their bedrooms turned into hell's extension.

What we buy from the devil is what we bring home. God always speaks to us through the Scripture by sounding the alarm bells of impending danger but most Christians do not heed to the warnings. It is sad that when a Christian is drawn to the desires of his heart, he turns away from Scriptural warnings.

Ten years of marriage produced six children in a hellish matrimonial home. The pastor this sister married was nothing but a crazy boxer who turned his beautiful wife into a punching bag. For a husband to turn his wife into a punching bag is a crime against the institution of marriage. But for a pastor to turn his matrimonial home into a boxing ring raises questions about his suitability as a leader of congregation. By way of personality and outer appearance, this pastor did not deserve the beautiful young woman he married. This is something I find difficult to understand of some women. My grandmother once said, "An ugly man who marries a beautiful woman will die of jealousy."

The young woman endured years of battering at the hands of the man she chose above all the men who asked for her hand in marriage. Every Sunday the wife came to Church trying to hide her swollen face, bruises, and black eyes or other horrendous injuries. Not wanting to expose her husband, she kept coming up with inconsistent, childish stories that made everyone draw his or her own conclusion as to the kind of husband she was married to.

Violent and abusive husbands are companions of the devil and women who tie the knot with such men are bound to suffer. It is my prayer that no woman will go to bed with such men who are nothing but tyrants. For a husband to turn his loving wife into a punching bag and demand she sleep with him shows he only married her for sex and nothing else. For this pastor to subject his wife to inhuman treatment only goes to show that God never called him to the ministry, which means he entered the ministry through the backdoor making him a thief.

One day the pastor came home late after a Church council meeting only to find an empty house and a note that read, "The children and I are gone forever. Do not look for us because you will never find us. I had to take this action to save myself from an untimely death at the hands of a tyrant like you and to prevent the children from further exposure to a violent home. You will never be missed."

The wife send a five-page A4 size dossier to the Bishop and the Church council detailing the reasons for her action. He was summoned before a disciplinary committee and told to respond the dossier and produce his wife and children. When he failed to produce his wife, children and respond to the dossier he was suspended from the Church and told his chances of ever returning to minister again in the Church were very remote.

This young woman has no one to blame but herself. She deliberately walked into a trap by deceiving herself that the man God chose for her was not God's will for her. When you invite the devil into your home, you end up marrying one of his children. In this woman's case that is exactly what she did. What this young woman did not know about the pastor she married was that he came from a culture where wife beating was acceptable as the norm. If she had taken time to explore the pastor's culture, she may not have married him. A pastor is like any ordinary person subject human weakness. Being married to a pastor does not guarantee you a happy marriage. A happy marriage depends on the character, attitude and behaviour of the person you are married to.

The pastor she married had all the qualities she was wanted in a man, so she turned down the man God had chosen for her. Marriage is never about outer appearance or personality because such qualities come with deception. A person's outer appearance can be very deceptive and blind us from sensing the toxic inside a person. The toxic in a person is what we can never see or sense in a person. It takes our daily walk with Christ and obedience to the Word of God to reveal the level of toxicity of the man or woman we want to marry.

Choosing a bride or bridegroom from the devil's world comes with the most deadly toxic. Similarly, if you choose a bride or a bridegroom from the church who is not the choice of God also comes with the most deadly toxic. If you fool yourself by believing Christians are non-toxic then you have no idea the kind of people who worship in the Church with you. Only God who sees what is inside a person can help us to avoid marrying toxic people in the church or outside the church. If you come to the church to look for a real Christian you will never find one. The life of a Christian outside the Church is the only way you can tell who a real Christian is. You can never tell who a real Christian is in the Church it is only when Christians are confronted by the realities of the outside world that we can know if they are made of toxic materials or non-toxic materials.

Health Issues: This is a very serious issue. Couples looking to get married should make it their major concern. Dating couples should learn each others medical history. Medical condition should override the love you have for each other. This is very important because if this is not known before marriage and you find out after the honeymoon that the person you have married is sick and cannot fulfil his or her marital role, there will be problems. In some instances, it has led to early divorce.

To illustrate this, I use the example of a very close friend. While at university she met a very handsome young law student. One day her boyfriend took her to visit his wealthy elder brother. As soon as she saw her fiancé's brother, she fell in love with him immediately. As a result, her attitude towards her fiancé changed.

She told her fiancée that she was no longer interested in him. When the boyfriend asked why, she said, "I like you very much, but when it comes to marriage it is your brother I love and not you. I like you, but I don't love you enough to marry you." But her fiancé would have none of this. As far as he was concerned they had come too far for them to end the relationship.

Perhaps the most painful statement a person can hear is, "I don't love you any more." Those words end relationships, break hearts and shatter dreams. Often people who have been betrayed guard themselves against future pain by deciding not to trust anyone's love again. A dreadful thing about this life is when a person vows to love you forever yet fails to keep that promise. But the good news in love is that God's love remains steadfast and sure. "He is the one who goes with you. He will not leave you nor forsake you" (Deut. 31:6).

All three in the love triangle were spirit-filled Christians and instead of them praying and seeking God's will for them they kept wrangling over a love issue that was beyond them. As a result, two brothers became entangled in an endless squabble over which of them the young woman really loved.

While this wrangling was going on, others were praying for God to give a sign as to which of them should marry the young woman. In answer to the prayers the young woman became sick and needed a blood transfusion. When they both turned up at the hospital as donors, the elder brother's blood was not compactable. But the younger brother, who was the young woman's fiancé, was a blood match to the young woman.

This was the first sign that God was working behind the scenes, but the problem is that sometimes we find it difficult to understand the way God works in our life. After the blood transfusion, two things happened. First, the young woman decided to marry her fiancé because it was he who donated the blood to save her life. Secondly, others concluded that the compatibility of the blood group indicated that it was God's answer that the young woman should marry her fiancé.

Nevertheless, as far as God was concerned, the reverse was true. God only intervened to reveal to them that what they did not know could cause problems if the girl and her fiancé were allowed to marry. During the blood screening it came to light that both the young woman and her fiancé had type **A S haemoglobin.** The doctor who carried out the blood transfusion advised the couple that their desire to marry could prove a disaster if they decided to have children.

He explained to them that possibility of their child or children being a carrier of the disease type **S S Sickle cell** disease was possible. What is sickle cell disease? Sickle Cell disease refers to a group of **inherited red blood cell disorder.** Sickle cell disease is not contagious; you cannot catch it. You inherit it from your parents. If, for example one parent has normal haemoglobin (type **A A**) and the second parents have abnormal haemoglobin **(type A S or Sickle Cell**

trait), there is a 50% chance that each child will have the **Sickle Cell trait,** but they will not have **Sickle Cell disease (type S S).**

If, however, both parents have type **A S haemoglobin** one normal and one abnormal, there is,

1. A 25% chance that the child will have **Sickle Cell disease.**
2. A 50% chance that the child will have **Sickle Cell trait.**
3. A 25% chance that the child will have neither the **disease nor trait.**

Health issues are what young couples planning to get married have to take a very serious view about in order to avoid future marital problems they cannot handle. It is much better for young, courting couples to understand that some medical conditions can impede a happy marital relationship irrespective of how we try to make things work. Here I am not talking about a medical condition that developed during marriage, rather about a medical condition you both know about before marriage. It is much better to break off an engagement and go your separate ways than allow yourselves to be bound by an unbreakable love that will one day turn a happy marriage into an unhappy marriage. Don't marry a person with a medical condition because of pity. A situation you know you cannot cope with is something every Christian should endeavour to avoid. It may seem for now that you can handle it, but the future is unpredictable and it could turn out to be a tragic mistake.

It is imperative that young, courting couples seek medical advice concerning known or unknown medical conditions before getting married. When it comes to choosing a life partner, Christians need to learn how to talk with God and reason in accordance with the Holy Spirit. We must learn to distinguish the voice of God from the voice of Satan, remember both of them may vie for your attention. The Holy Spirit will never tell us to do something in relation to each other that He Himself does not do for us.

CULTURAL BELIEF

A person's culture has so much influence on him or her that he or she tends to be drawn towards people of his own culture. This may not always be the case; however, the chances are that he or she is more likely o blend into his own community. Love can break cultural barriers but it cannot do away with customs and traditions. Love complements custom and traditions rather than breaking away from them.

It is imperative that in a cosmopolitan society, consenting adults who fall in love with people of different cultures should endeavour to study carefully the cultural of the man or woman they want to marry. Being careful to exploit the customs and traditions of your fiancée may turn out to be what will one day save your marriage. We must not underestimate the way culture influences human behaviour.

The most important thing in every culture has to do with **what is considered right and wrong.** In a cosmopolitan society, our ability to gain insight into others' culture will be crucial in cementing good relationships. After all, a Cosmopolitan society is supposed be the kind of society that should blend people of different races or ethnic groups together and does not segregate them.

The way things are done: these deals with what are regarded in customs and traditions as the norm. For example, in giving away daughters in marriage, every culture has a procedure to be followed by the groom's parents before the marriage can be recognised. Rules are regarded as the most important in every culture.

Therefore, for cross-cultural marriage to work, people of different cultures who fall in love and want to marry will have to discover this. A desire to discover the customs and traditions of your fiancé will place you at the very centre of your future in-laws. This desire will make your future in-laws feel you want to be part of their culture.

It gives the impression that you are not only marrying into the family, but willing to be married to the culture and be part of it. Marrying into your spouse's culture simply means you are willing to accept their customs and traditions respect them and are willing to blend into their culture. To be married to a person of a different culture and to be devoid of his or her culture will make in-laws have second thought about your intentions.

If you love your fiancée, then you should be willing to love his or her culture, customs and traditions. His people become your people. Turning to the Scripture gives us a classical example of how to fit into your spouse's culture. The story of Ruth portrays a woman who married not for only love, but also loved the culture of her husband.

When Ruth's mother in-law asked her to go back to her people and culture she replied, "Don't urge me to leave you or turn back from you. Where you go I will go and where you stay, I will stay. Your people will be my people and your God will be my God. Where you die I will die, and there I will be buried." (Ruth 1:16-17)

We must recognise that every culture has an element of pride. The last thing your spouse would want is for you to look down on his or her culture. When in-laws pick-up the slightest signal that shows you have no respect or regard for their culture, this can create tension in the marriage.

Again we must recognise that every culture has an element of good and evil. Therefore, spouses who have married outside their culture should endeavour to make the culture of their spouse a part of their cultural value and behaviour.

Within the framework of married life, customs and traditions should serve as a binding cord in the marriage and not drive spouses away from each other. When a husband's cultural truth is faithfully and lovingly applied to the wife's culture, the result will be an amalgamated culture. However, culture must be tested and judged to remove the unhealthy element within the custom and its tradition.

In a Multicultural society, marriage can either bridge cultural boundaries or divide cultures. Is cosmopolitan society the answer to cross-cultural marriage? Has the cosmopolitan society the power to dislodge conservatives and traditionalist who oppose cross-cultural marriage? The answer to these questions can be found in human traditions. Tradition is the catalyst that has stalled the drive towards some cross-cultural marriage.

To fully understand the subject of cross-cultural marriage we must understand the meaning of the following terms: **Culture, Tradition, customs, communication and multi-culture.** These words will help to get an insight of the subject matter. These words differ from country to country and even within a country, they have different meanings.

On the other hand, we will examine critically the three great religions of the world and their views of cross-cultural marriage that are embedded in customs and traditions. We cannot treat the subject of cross-cultural without the issue of religious belief. The human race is bound either by their religion or culture.

The clash of these two can sometimes have profound consequences on any marriage. It is like driving a wedge between two trains of gears in a mesh. Those blinded by love and think they can tear down both **religion barriers and cultural barriers** to marry because of love should first study the word Love: as defined by each of the three great religions of the world.

The three great religions of the world are **Judaism, Christianity and Islam.** We will look at each of them and then examine the views of each of them in the light of cross-cultural marriage. We will look at taboos in the light of these three great religions. It may be possible in some instances for love to tear down cultural barriers to enable couples who are passionately in love to marry. However, when it comes to religious marriage, this may not be the case. With religious faith, the consequences of crossing religions can be high.

There are so many religions in the world but these three religions of the Middle East have been chosen because they all believe in the existence of one God. On the other hand, we have **Hinduism and Sikhism** as the religions of India, **Taoism, Confucianism, Buddhism and Shintoism** as the religions of the Eastern Asia.

CULTURE

Every man is king of his own castle: This is what you may not know about certain cultures. Fear of women learning to assert themselves is nothing new as the account of Esther shows. Queen Vashti's refusal to parade her beauty at her husband's men only, week-long drinking-fest (Esther 1:5-12) was officially interpreted as nothing less than an act of rebellion against male authority (1:16-17). As a result, King Ahasuerus fired off a decree intended to reinforce the mastery of every male in the empire over the women (1:22).

It would be perilous to try to judge ancient cultures and customs against modern-day understanding of gender issues. Nevertheless, it seems clear that some of the men of Persia felt threatened by Vashti's self-will. Perhaps they feared the social chaos that might result if women refused to comply with their husband's wishes, no matter how degrading those wishes might be.

Many men today display similar fears about assertive and independent women. The Book of Esther can help by showing the value of a woman with strong character. Vashti's successor, Esther, also showed assertiveness by not waiting to be called by Ahasuerus, but entering into his presence at the risk of her life (4:11; 5:1-3). Even in to day's world some culture are male dominated and turn to keep women to looking after children and house hold activities.

The Oxford Advanced Learner's Dictionary defines culture as, "The way of life and social organization of a particular country or group with its own beliefs." The idea that our traits are better than the cultural traits of other is one reason why some oppose cross-cultural marriage. The whole of a culture is made up of many aspects like food, religion and attitude.

An individual's culture encloses him completely just as a capsule containing medication is completely enclosed by a plastic-like material. A person is enclosed inside his culture like a plastic covering. We become made aware of our cultural enclosure by the attitude and actions of other people regarding us rather than from our own consciousness.

For example, Kwame, when asked why he often takes Ghanaian food to Europe, he said, "I want to live in Europe like the way I have seen Europeans live in Ghana." It is very true that when a person migrates to another country he wants to maintain his cultural identity. It is part of the human character to reject strange cultures.

You walk the streets of England, France and Germany and you will notice Jewish shops, African shops, Arab shops, South American shops, Pilipino shops and Indian shops, Chinese shops. The question we should be asking is; are these people not interested in European staple food? The answer is simple. These migrants are all encased in their cultural capsules. Have you notice that when America tourists travel to different part of the world they look for restaurants that serve them hot dogs. You will find them patronizing MacDonald's and Starbuck shops.

People who maintain their cultural identity grow to become conscious of their family relationships; this creates strong ties in the family. People make ties through arranged marriage between families and communities. On the other hand, families do not marry to establish relationship. Family ties strengthen bond between families.

In Cross-cultural marriage you cannot marry a person without becoming involved in his or her culture. If you marry a woman you marry her with her culture in the same way if you are married to a man you are also married to his culture. A person and his culture are inseparable because a person grows with his or her culture.

From the very first day a newborn baby takes his or her first breath that child is initiated into his or her culture. His culture becomes part of his way of thinking, his way of living and the way of doing things. His behaviour portrays his culture. His culture introduces him to the staple diet and he grows up to like familiar food associate to his culture.

Every food can be identified with a particular Culture. For example, at the mere mention of the word **Pizza** and the finger points to Italian staple food, an Italian dish consisting of a flat round bread base with cheese, tomatoes, vegetables and meat. Again, mention the word **curry** and everybody knows it is an Indian staple dish of meat and vegetables, cooked with hot spices, often served with rice.

At the mention of the word **couscous** and every body knows is a type of North African food made from crushed wheat; a dish made of meat and /or vegetable with couscous. You mention the word **sushi** and it's a Japanese dish of small cake of cold cooked rice, flavoured with vinegar served with raw fish.

Del Tarr, in his book Cross-Cultural Communication used French, English and American way of eating to denote cultural differences. He wrote: "The French are noted for their great appreciation of food. They spend much time in its preparation and like to spend a long time in its consumption. The English and the Americans are much simpler in their attitude toward food and consider too much emphasis on feeding the body to be sinful."

In France it is common for most important meal of the day to be eaten at noon. The house wife spends most of the morning in getting the noon meal ready for the family. Most stores and shop in France close down at noon so that the shoppers and owners can rush home at noon to eat a leisurely meal that has been well prepared and is often very delightful to the senses.

An American considers the noon meal to be only a small lunch and often carries it to work with him in a brown paper bag. The lunchtime for the average worker in America is between thirty and forty-five minutes, and some take only a few minutes to eat their sandwiches quickly. The Frenchman will take two hours to eat a leisurely meal and then rest a few moments to allow the food to digest before going back to work in the afternoon.

You can imagine the potential communication problems surrounding this variation in the habits of eating. The French have a way of mentally stopping time before the shrine of good food. The American visiting France sees this as a waste of time and the Frenchman's fixation with food as sinful or sensuous, or at least strange. The Frenchman believes that his American counterpart lacks cultural values and has no appreciation for the finer things of life.

These examples, brings out a person's **cultural heritage** into the limelight of cross-cultural marriage. Heritage is a tradition and qualities that a country or society has had for many years and that are considered an important part of its character. African's rich cultural heritage can be found in the way of dressing. We will look at this in detail later under the heading Custom.

In today's modern multi-cultural society, young people think culture does not play any important role in cross-cultural marriage. Sorry, it does because we all have families and every family is tied to its culture. This we cannot break away from. The moment we recognized we have a family then we have a culture and our roots are buried in our culture.

The story of Matilda can be used as an example: she is a stunning young Turkish woman married to an Englishman. This story is a typical example of the clash in cross-cultural marriage. However, it also represents a typical example of a wonderful cross-cultural marriage. The only thing that sometimes mars this happy marriage is what we call **Cross-cultural respect.**

Cross-Cultural respect: It is the acknowledgment of a person's cultural heritage or acknowledging that a person's has a culture and his or her cultural must be accepted, respected and honoured. It represents a mark of respect for a person's cultural heritage. Our failure to recognise and respect the culture of our spouse can create problems in the marriage.

Respect-The Oxford Advance Learners Dictionary has several definitions for the word respect, but for the purpose of this book, we will limit ourselves to that which will bring a clearer understanding or will help us to understand the word **respect** in respect of cross-cultural marriage.

Respect, to be careful about; to make sure you do not; that should be consider to be wrong. The word respect may have different understanding from one culture to the other, because what one culture may consider being respectful another culture may consider it not an important issue.

A clash of cultural marriage is what threatened Matilda's marriage. It all started from the day she got married and her in-laws started to visit. Any time Matilda's in-laws came to visit, she addressed them as Mum and Dad. She never called her husband's parents by their names because of her cultural upbringing. Her culture dictated that spouses address each other's parents as mum and dad. In some cultures, it is disrespectful for a man or woman to call their in-laws by their names; however some consider it correct to addressing their in-laws by their real names.

When Matilda's parents came to visit, her English husband addressed her parents by their names and this upset them, a **case of cross-cultural disrespect.** But their son in-law did not see anything wrong in calling his wife's parents by their names. Here, it is obvious Matilda's husband is encased in his cultural capsule. The reason for this behaviour is simple; he is looking at things from his own cultural perspective, and this is where he is wrong. When a husband approaches his in-law from his own cultural perspective, it is deemed culturally incorrect. The behaviour of Matilda's husband illustrates a man uninformed about his wife's culture.

His in-laws regarded his attitude towards them as disrespectful because they did not understand why their son in-law cannot address them as mum and dad, when their daughter addresses his parents as mum and dad. To keep the peace in a cross-cultural marriage sometimes it is worth looking beyond our own cultural values and see what other cultures regard as **Cultural Ethic.**

In cross-cultural marriage, breaking free from the cultural capsule that encases us will help to bring peace in our marriage. Coming out of the cultural capsule that encases us does not mean we have to leave it altogether. We only do so when our spouse's **cultural ethics** demands that.

Do not use the standard of your culture to measure other people's culture or use your cultural ethics to judge other cultures. In dealing with people of different culture you must not look at them with your cultural mirror. Rather, look at them from their own cultural mirror. For example, in some cultures the role of a woman in a marriage is that of cooking for the family cleaning, washing and childbearing, while the men are the breadwinners. Do you know that in some cultures it is women who pay the bride-price?

With issues of cultural perspective we must understand that talking to our spouses about our culture more often can help put our own culture into perspective. Every culture has moral principle or moral values based on a system of moral beliefs about what they belief is right or wrong. When we cross the cultural line designed to uphold the cultural values we find ourselves in **contempt of culture.** This then becomes a deliberate disrespect of your spouse's culture.

When we look at ourselves in our own cultural mirror, we will end up offending other people's culture. This is exactly what this young man was doing. Spouses in cross-cultural marriage must endeavour to look at themselves in both cultural mirrors because in cross-cultural marriage two cultures are intertwining.

In the Western world, it is considered correct for a son in-law or daughter-in-law to call their in-laws by their names. In most families you only refer to your own parents as mum and dad. As children grow they watch and follow the behaviour Pattern of their culture and consider it the norm. A standard of behaviour that is accepted within a particular group may be deemed disrespectful by another culture.

One could say that the cultural values held by any given people can differ from any other people's worldview. Traditionalists who assume that their culture is faultless and does not need changing will not understand clearly when people advocate for change. Nevertheless, changes must be allowed; they should happen slowly and should not destroy cultural values.

Some cultures would tolerate change with some reluctance. However, traditionalists reject cultural change because they see reformists as people who regard custom and traditions as old and outdated. In cross-cultural marriage, we have to tread carefully so as not to offend in-laws who regard themselves as custodians of customs and traditions.

For example, Juliet is English married to an Englishman, she calls her in-laws by their real names when I asked why, this is what she said, "They are not my parents and I cannot call them mum and dad." This statement is correct within Western culture where a son-in-law or daughter-in-law could address their in-law by their names. However, in certain cultures it can be seen as a disrespectful.

What a contrast. Failure to understand your spouse's culture with regard to the word respect is an unpardonable offence. Let us now turn to the Holy Scripture to help us put the words cultural respect in their correct perspective. We must understand that the Bible was written in the culture of those to whom the Scripture was first addressed.

In Romans Chapter 14, Verses 19 to 21 Paul writes, "Let us therefore make every effort to do what leads to peace and mutual edification. Do not destroy the work of God for the sake of food. All food is clean, but it is wrong for a man to eat anything that causes someone else to stumble. It is better not to eat meat or drink wine or to do anything else that will cause your brother to fall."

Certain cultures forbid the eating of certain meats. This has nothing to do with religious faith. The abstaining from certain meat has to do with a taboo that has been handed down from generation to generations. Fear is the underlying reason why such taboos have a strong hold on some cultures.

Those who find themselves in cross-cultural marriage must learn what the culture of their spouse regards as acceptable behaviour and what unacceptable behaviour is. There is therefore no excuse for ignorance for failing to respect the culture of your spouse. You cannot claim to love your spouse and yet be ignorant of his or her culture.

In another example, is of a Ghanaian married to German woman. When his mother came to visit her son and her daughter-in-law for the first time, what she saw shocked her beyond belief. When she saw her son cooking and washing plates, she said, "I am finished! Western marriage has turned my son into a woman. This woman will kill my son." Culturally, she is right in making such a statement because she was looking at things from her own cultural mirror.

This woman is completely encased in her own culture capsule. She concluded that Western culture has enslaved her son and reduced him to the role of a woman. This woman was looking at things in her cultural mirror. As a result she has become blinded by what her cultural regard as the norm.

In Africa, the Middle East and Asia, cultures regard the kitchen as a woman's world and not a place for a man. Therefore, what she was witnessing was a taboo because it is not accepted in her culture for a married man to cook and wash dishes in the home. However, in the Western society there is nothing culturally wrong with the husband cooking and washing dishes.

We call this a clash of cross-cultural marriage. She found herself in a strange country with a strange culture that had no respect for what her culture regarded as the norm for the institution of marriage. Frustrated and powerless to effect change, she turned to her husband to instil their cultural values in their son's marriage.

Her daughter-in-law on the other hand, did not see why this should be an issue. Here, she was behaving within her cultural norm. This implies she was looking through her own cultural mirror. As far as she was concerned, there was nothing wrong with her watching television whilst her African husband prepares dinner. This is where she too is wrong, because she is insensitive to what her husband's culture regards as acceptable behaviour. If she familiarized herself with her husband's cultural beliefs this unpleasant situation could be have been avoided.

If this young woman had taken interest in educating herself in her husband's culture, she could have saved an embarrassing situation. If she had taken a keen interest in the cultural orientation of her husband, she could have established a strong bond with her mother in-law. This woman's lack of interest in her husband's culture nearly caused a rift between her and her mother in-law.

Knowing that her mother in-law was coming for a visit should have given her ample time to know the role of an African woman in marriage and adapted to it. She should have known things like how to address her mother in-law, what her mother in-law would be expecting of her and how to conduct herself culturally so as not to offend her husband's culture.

In her husband's culture; a woman wakes up in the morning to prepare breakfast for her husband before he goes to work. Then when the husband comes home, she gets the bath ready for him' then the husband sits comfortably waiting to be served with his dinner. When the husband finishes eating, the wife collects the plates and washes them while the husband sits with a toothpick in his mouth.

On the other hand, what the African woman did not know was that both her son and daughter-in-law are professionals with demanding jobs. As a result, whoever came home first will have to fix dinner. The housework is shared between the husband and the wife and this arrangement brings peace and harmony in the home without overworking either of them.

The above arrangement could be offensive in a culture that regard cooking and housework as a woman's duty. In a modern society where married couple work long hours to pay bills, raise children and put food on the table, the issue of who does the cooking and housework should have nothing to do with culture. The African woman was culturally blind to her daughter-in-law's culture.

For cross cultural marriage to work in our modern day society we have to examine our culture in the light of multicultural society and accept that which will be compatible in marriage and reject that which is old. Nevertheless, we cannot ignore our culture but we can modernize it.

Some cultures have outlived their usefulness in this modern society because in many ways they stand in the way of progress. They also create cultural barriers that add to intolerance. We can only succeed in bringing about gradual changes to culture by looking at what needs changing through the mirror of our culture. That's only if we are willing to come out of the cultural capsule and see that the world around us is changing rapidly.

Marriage is about love, and culture should not be an obstacle in the way of two people in love. Culture should never be a barrier to marriage in a cosmopolitan society. If it is then such a culture needs reforming. In an age where people travel to all over the globe they are bound to fall in love with people of different cultures and races.

Nevertheless, our culture is our identity and everywhere we go people only have to look are at the way we dress, our dialect and the way we do things and they can tell where we come from. However, in our quest to marry we must be careful we do not ignore what our culture deems as the acceptable way of doing things. This is all-important because it leads to peace and harmony between both cultures.

There are certain cultures which do not accept cross-cultural marriage because of their perception of it. Their view of cross-cultural marriage is that it will affect the upbringing of children. Here their perception is culturally incorrect, because of the merits of raising children in two different cultures. For example, children born out of two cultures have the advantage of being bilingual; have dual nationality and benefiting from learning about both cultures.

Nadia is a young Liberal Moslem from Cyprus. At college, she fell in love with an English man. Her parents said nothing negative about their relationship, but deep down they wished it hadn't happened because they considered the relationship unholy. When her boyfriend proposed to her, he was confronted by a culture that would not accept such marriages.

Her parents brought up the issue of cultural boundaries by telling them, "We cannot approve of such a marriage because our cultural beliefs are bound to be in conflict with your cultural values." This kind of statement is what we call a cultural barrier. What her parents should be concerned about is whether the young man would love, cherish and take good care of their daughter.

The parents use an outdated code of cultural conduct that should never have been an issue to erect a barrier between the young man and his girlfriend. Love must always override cultural differences. The primary ingredient in every marriage is love and not cultural values. Culture is good, but when it becomes a stumbling block in marriage it leaves many people bitter.

In cross-cultural marriage we have to look at what must be seen as **logical necessity** and what should be regarded as **personal obligation.** Here love speaks of the former and culture is associated with the latter. Nevertheless, culture plays a significant role in traditional marriage and we should never lose sight of this.

1. **Logical necessity:** speaks of love that binds two people together, with each willing to die for the other.
2. **Personal obligation:** speaks of personal interest that interferes with other's interest. It seeks self at the expense of others. It does not feel what others are going through.

In a multicultural society, strong bonds are built between different cultures strong opposition by those who see marriage within a culture as a means preserving cultural heritage. In fact, if you study the reasons why some people oppose cross-cultural marriage you will find that it has nothing to do with culture, but rather to do with racial segregation.

In the ancient world, rulers used marriage as a way to seal treaties, alliance and other covenants. History has taught has that peace treaties were signed by kings and sealed with marriage to guarantee the continuity of peace between kingdoms. These marriages were cross-cultural marriage designed for peace and harmony between Kingdoms. Kings gave their daughters or sisters in marriage to seal peace treaties.

From the above we can conclude that cross-cultural marriage existed from the first centuries and has continued to this day. In those days, cross-cultural marriage served as olive branch that led to peace among Kingdoms. The cross-cultural marriage between Kingdoms served as a reminder of peace treaties. Therefore, they became known as Political marriage.

The wonderful institution of marriage God gave the human race has become a peace process to prevent war between two Kingdoms. Whatever God has given us is good for us, if only we knew how to use it as God intended. The intended purpose of the marriage institution is what we need to understand.

When we fail to understand the intended purpose of the institution of marriage and lose track of it then we end up dragging marriage into muddy waters. Marriage is a wonderful gift from God and we must do everything to preserve the joy, happiness and the peace that comes with it. When we honour our marriage, we honour God because He created the institution of marriage.

Nevertheless, human cultures and customs are very good to humanity because they serve as a guiding principle for moral behaviour and cultural ethics. They set the code of conduct for marriage, childcare, respect for elders, and pattern of behaviour, how kings and queens are enthroned and dethroned and how Political leaders are to govern their subjects.

In cross-cultural marriage we need to investigate what the culture we are marrying into regards as the norm. When it comes to divorce, cultures differ in what they regard as the due process of separation and divorce. In some cultures, divorce does not favour women and women have to investigate this thoroughly before committing themselves.

Iran, for example, is a country whose culture does not favour women when it comes to divorce. The culture states that when couples can no longer live together and they decide to divorce, the woman takes custody of the children as long as she does not remarry. But if she decides to remarry, she loses custody of the children to her husband.

This system of settling divorce is open exploitation for abusive husbands who are keen on walking away with everything in the marriage. For example, an unfaithful husband who wants to get rid of his wife to marry his mistress and still keep his children can wreck havoc in the marriage. That can force the wife to initiate divorce proceedings.

What makes this system unfair is that if the wife is the one who initiates the divorce proceedings, she forfeits any right to claim anything in the marriage. This means she loses everything. And even if the husband remarries, the wife can only keep the children as long as she remains single. Nevertheless, if it is the husband who initiates the divorce, then the wife is entitled to claim compensation.

Children, the joy of marriage are often forgotten and sidelined until the two people in the divorce battle have satisfied their selfish interest. The tragic thing about this kind of divorce is that children who are the centre of affection in marriage could sometimes be given custody to a violent father who may be alcoholic and abusive.

In all divorce cases where children are involved, the children's interest should override cultural beliefs, customs and traditions. But it is sad that many traditional divorce courts ignore the welfare of the children when awarding custody. The world is changing very fast, and this has affected people's lifestyle, behaviour, the way they think about things and the way they approach things.

Custom and tradition need to change to reflect the changing cosmopolitan society. In world where the youth are turning their back to customs and tradition, the custodians of culture should find a way of refining customs and traditions that will appeal to an emerging generation that find customs and traditions to be something of the past. Cultures, tradition and customs need refining to be in-line with modern day cosmopolitan society. This means a thorough overhaul of culture.

CUSTOMS

Customs - Is defined as an accepted way of behaving or doing things in a community. Every society has rules for giving their daughters away in marriage. For example, according to the custom of Wodaabe people of Niger, any marriage that is not prearranged by parents could be regarded as abduction. In some countries, the groom's parents pay a bride price. In other countries, it is the bride's parents who pay the groom's price before the marriage is fulfilled.

In India, and some Middle Eastern countries, it is common practice that the bride's parents pay the groom's parents money as their customs demands before the marriage can be consummated. A person coming from a country where the groom's parents pay the bride's price will fine these customs very strange.

Each culture has a way performing customary rites before their daughters can be married. One example is the Krobo people of Eastern Ghana. It is their custom that when a young girl reaches the age of puberty, she has to undergo a traditional initiation into womanhood before she can be married.

This traditional initiation is called "Dipo," where young girls are adorned in beautiful traditional costumes and parade through the street singing and dancing to the tunes of traditional drummers. It is very splendid to watch these stunning young girls walk proudly into womanhood for the first time in their lives.

The puberty rites are held every year between the months of April and May and last for a period of four days. They are restricted from eating however they are allowed to drink water from a well. The girls are taught the Kloma dance, and undergo a ritual bath. The crux of the rite is when they are made to sit on a stone which it is believed, determines virginity. Any girl who is found not to be a virgin at the time of the rites used to be ostracized in the past and was treated as an outcast. However, nowadays a set of purification are performed to replace the old system, thanks to a reformist who advocated for change to meet the new order of the twenty-first century. In a world where it has become very difficult to find virgins, the custodians of customs and tradition have no choice but to reform in order to conform what today's society regards as the norm.

On the day of the ceremony the initiate will be ready for the ceremony, during which they will be presented to the community of family friends and potential suitors. The joy of the initiations is shared with the parents of the girl and immediate family. It is taboo for a young woman to be married without going through the initiation and would bring shame to the members of the girl's family.

Customs are like instilling discipline in a child, from birth so when the child grows up he or she does not deviate from what is known as right and wrong. Every child is born into a custom and parents become the custodians with the responsibility of instilling the customs into the child as he or she grows.

There is the barbaric practice of female circumcision (Female Genital Mutilation). This practice is associated with the religion of Islam; this is the view of researchers. I strongly disagree with this idea because the practice of FGM was in existence long before Islam was founded by Mohamed. Therefore, it has nothing to do with any of the three great religions of the Middle East; rather it has to do with custom in the area.

There is strong evidence that when people accept a new religious faith they try to incorporate their customs into the new religion in order to make it acceptable to their way of living. This is one of the deceptive ploys by the devil to make people believe customs can be amalgamated into religion. Religion and customs are two different things: you cannot marry the two together. Marrying of customs and religion produces something that is neither true region nor false religion but in the end it leads to idol worship in disguise. The product of such faith can keep its worshipers in darkness, because the truth is obscured from them.

Female circumcision is barbaric, evil and its ritual is satanic. This is the view of majority of people interviewed. They are of the view that such a custom should be outlawed in this modern generation. A new world order is taking place in this civilized century and such a custom has no place in it. It would be worth making changes to certain customs in order to keep the good ones and discard the bad ones.

For example, I know a Christian woman from Sierra-Leone, who said that the idea behind female circumcision is devilish and has something to do with witchcraft. She said the night before she and her sisters were circumcised they were locked in a room and prevented from going out. They stayed in there till the following morning and taken out of the room one after other for the circumcision.

When it was her turn, she put up a fierce struggle with the women who came for her. She somehow managed to escape but she was chased down and overpowered, and brought back to the room where the circumcision was taking place. Then four women pinned her down and opened her legs wide apart. Then a woman approached her with a blade and cut her. She said, as soon as the woman started cutting her she collapsed with her head falling back. From that day on she was never the same woman she knew herself to be.

She has never forgiven her father who ordered the circumcision or the women who shamed her pride by deforming her. Her mother, who was a Christian, vehemently opposed the circumcision, but she was overruled by her husband who was a devout Muslim. This should be a lesson for Christians who thinks there is nothing wrong with a Christian marrying from a different religion. It was only when she became a Christian that she was able to forgive them.

The word **syncretism** means the combination of two different beliefs. For example, to the animist, it is the mixing of Biblical doctrines with animistic beliefs and rituals. Even after an animist has accepted Jesus as his personal Saviour, he will often be tempted to merge his new belief with his animist beliefs. (See *People and Their Beliefs* by Paul Wright).

People who come from countries that do not practice FGM should be aware of this before marrying people from countries who see FGM as part of their custom. I know of a West African woman married to a man from the Caribbean who took her two daughters to her native town and came home with her daughters circumcised. The enraged husband called in the social service, who involved the police.

In cross-cultural marriage, we must be sensitive to our spouse's culture and strike a balance between what should be accepted as custom and what should be rejected as an evil and barbaric practice. What should be noted in every marriage is love and not customs. However, customs must be respected but not at the expense of love.

When it comes to customs, we must be very careful because certain practices clash with religious beliefs. This can become problematic in cross-cultural marriage. A person's customs go deep into his or her heart, and he or she has been brought up to believe that it is the acceptable way of doing things.

Do you know that in many cultures Polygamy is cultural accepted? Since this practice is deeply ingrained within their culture, they do not see it as violating a social norm. Therefore, they do not regard it as disrupting family values. Polygamy has existed since marriage began and its continuation has become part of certain customs.

In cultures where polygamy is practiced, men whose wives are unable to bear children are pressurised by their parents to take a second wife. Parents desperate for grandchildren will stop at nothing to lure their son into a Polygamous marriage. Polygamy then becomes important to child bearing in cultures that regard male children as the only means of continuing the family linage.

In cross-cultural marriage, traditional and customs can be very good where both spouse's customs are welded together. This can only take place when the husband and wife are both liberal. However, if either of them is conservative then it will be very difficult to work toward a compromise.

The problem here is that love can blind people and prevent them from knowing certain things about their fiancée's custom before they get married. Customs and tradition are very important in today's multicultural society. It is something we cannot brush it aside. For example, an Asian friend invited me to a wedding party where most people were dressed in traditional Indian dress. The marriage ceremony itself was conducted according Indian customs.

It will interest you to know that despite the bride and bridegroom being born in a multicultural society they were both dressed in Indian traditional dress. The question we should ask is why did the bride and the bridegroom dress as their customs dictate; why was the marriage conducted according to the customs of the couple? The answer is simple; this was done to remind the bride and the bridegroom of their roots. Migrants, in fear of their children losing their customs and traditions instil their customs into their children from an early age. Their aim is that their children will pass the customs and traditions on from generation to generation, in this way the continuity of the custom is guaranteed.

When it comes to marriage, customs and traditions cannot be ignored because they form part of the marriage ceremony. Without customs and traditions there would be no marriage ceremony and if there was no marriage ceremony, then there would be no marriage. The roots of marriage are buried in custom and traditions.

TRADITION

Before we define the meaning of tradition we will look at the word **Ethnocentrism, i**t will help us to understand what tradition really is and why it is difficult to break away from tradition. Del Tarr in his book (*Cross-Cultural Communication*) explains Ethnocentrism as a form of opposition to change that causes a person or a people to practice wilful cultural isolation.

He uses the behaviour of a Paraguayans in the U S to illustrate a classical example of Ethnocentric. He used an article that was published in an El Salvador newspaper. He wrote, "These excerpts were published as an editorial in that newspaper. Here is a loose translation of them from Spanish." Now read on.

I have just received this letter from my Celerion Menchaca, my excellent Paraguayan friend who has lived in New York City for thirty years without working and without Celerion Menchaca learning to talk English. Menchaca writes, 'People have asked me infinity of times why I have lived these many years in the United State without becoming a naturalized citizen. I have not become a naturalized U.S for various reasons, the principal reasons being that of reciprocity. What I mean is; **I wish to live here like I have often seen the North American live overseas.**

Tradition is defined as a way of doing things that has existed for a long time among a particular group of people. For example, to break a tradition to get married secretly without the knowledge of the custodians can result in a marriage not being accepted by elders of the family. The couple may be regarded as outcasts.

Tradition can also be defined as "the handing down of information, beliefs, and custom by word of mouth or by example from one generation to another without written instruction." Many traditions are good and necessary and they serve to bind people into a common society that helps them work and live together.

In Niger, the Wodaabe people continue to preserve their traditions and taboos of the past. Prohibitions imposed upon their behaviour is rigid. For example: During daylight a man cannot hold his wife's hand in public, call her by name, or speak to her in a personal way. Parents may never talk directly to their first - and second-born children or refer to them by name.

However, many traditions are useless, and serve to provide walls or boundaries between neighbours and even friends. For example, think of the traditions in the days of Jesus. In the story of the Good Samaritan, we see a man that cut through all the traditions and prejudice of the day to help a man in trouble. He did this even though he was from a culture that said, "Jews and Samaritan have no dealings."

The two have never got on well enough to help each other. The Samaritan, however, saw the need and reached out in love and helped the needy. Have you today come to a crossroad where you are faced with a tradition that is hindering you from marrying the man or woman you love? Many traditions have kept young couples passionately in love from even talking to each other, let alone marrying.

In some cultures, tradition demands that couples intending to marry get the blessing of the parent and the elders of the family. Failing to get the blessing of the family can result in the couple being cursed by elders of the family. The only solution to this is what is known as the **traditional marriage.** As far as traditionalists are concerned traditional marriage is very important.

Therefore the traditionalist attaches so much importance to traditional marriage that they regard it as a prerequisite to a Church wedding. Traditional marriage is the form of marriage that existed before the Western Church wedding was introduced to non - Western society through Christianity. It is very difficult for people to break free from their method of ratifying marriage.

It is very important that the youth today must endeavour to go through traditional marriage before Church weddings are conducted to avoid certain repercussions that might follow. Some cultures do not recognize church wedding without the couples going through traditional weddings. A church wedding without a traditional marriage is seen as a snub to customs and traditions.

In some cultures, tradition does not allow women to get pregnant outside wedlock or cohabit. Men who hold traditions in high esteem may disown their daughters if they become pregnant outside of wedlock. Traditionalists regard pregnancy out off wed-lock as bringing shame to the family name.

Tradition is like attitude; a person's attitude can tell us who he or she really is. It is evident that people do not change easily or quickly. Similarly, traditions do not change overnight. Certain traditions can be slightly changed to meet our modern worldview.

A very good friend called Singh is married to a beautiful young woman from Bulgaria. During their courtship, he told his fiancée, "I want you to know who I am, what I am and what my culture is. Therefore, I am taking you to India for you to get to know my people and to study the kind of marriage you are getting into before you make any commitment."

He made his fiancée aware that in the Sikh religion, a woman is not only married to her husband but also to his family. If she is willing to accept the traditional Sikh way of marriage, then nothing can stop them from marrying. She accepted the trial marriage proposal and after six months, they got married in a Sikh Temple.

The marriage was conducted according to Sikh traditions. There was not a single hint of Western flavour in the ceremony. One would have thought by combining Asian and Western cultural flavours into the marriage, one would see a beautiful picture of cross-cultural marriage.

However, she made him aware that she was not going to accept all the customs, especially customs that would infringe on her cultural beliefs. The family gave careful thought of their daughter in-law's request and concluded that in the interest of respect for her culture she should be allowed to ignore Sikh customs that would infringe on her religious beliefs and lead to problems in the marriage.

For example, converting to the Sikh religion would not be an obligation but a personal choice, if she wanted to. She would be allowed to keep her Roman Catholic faith without the family interfering. None of them would impose their faith on the children. Instead, they would introduce the children to both faiths and allow them to make a personal decision when they are old enough to make that choice.

We must be very careful we are not drawn into such a marriage because of love. Rather, we should look beyond love into the future to ensure that the decision you make today, does not come back to hunt you. Cross-cultural marriage comes with its own problems.

Therefore, we have to study the cultures of each other by introducing your culture to your spouse for him or her to know the culture of the spouse they are marrying. What we must know is **certain traditions do not favour women.** Therefore, women should examine their spouse culture very carefully before committing themselves into a marriage that will turn out nothing but regret.

If a man really loves his fiancée, he will not allow outdated traditions to stand in her way. A tradition that reduces women to the rank of slaves has no place in the Twenty-First century. The **Holy Bible recognizes men and women as equal partners in marriage.** The Scriptures does not place the wife as a subordinate to her husband. Women have to be very careful and not be fooled by love.

Of what use will it be if you marry a man you love passionately only for his culture render you insignificant in the marriage. I know of a young couple from West Africa who met in America while they were studying in the same university. They fell in love without checking each other's cultural background, although they came from the same country.

When they came home at the end of the studies, they were confronted with the realities of a cultural divide. Traditionalists invoked an old law that bars the two cultures from marrying. While the young man came from a royal family the young woman came from a lower cast system of culture. When the couple decided to marry, they were told they could not because it was taboo.

When the couple could not tear down the cultural barrier, the young woman went back to America while the young man stayed behind. He met and fell in love with a rich man's daughter. After eight months' courtship, he married the young woman in a colourful wedding. Cultural barriers are sometimes difficult to pull down as long as conservative elders are determined to uphold the cultural values. Traditional elders regard themselves as custodians of cultural values and will not relent until they see that customs and traditions handed down from generation to generations are upheld by their children. Traditionalist everywhere regards themselves as enforcers of traditions.

We must not resent traditionalist who try to retain the cultural values of their customs and traditions. Without them, some cultures would be lost forever. Let's take South America, for example; there are some South American countries that have lost their language. The only language they can speak and write is Spanish. These people have no languages to teach the coming generations. The good news is that in the mist of lost cultural language they have managed to keep their traditions and customs intact, although some of them have been blended with Western culture.

MULTICULTURE

A multicultural society is defined as people of several different races, religions, languages and traditions living together. However, this does not mean that people living in a multicultural do not have separate identities. Many people living in a multicultural society want to maintain separate identity.

In fact, "multicultural" is more of a political word these days. The term is used by politicians to win votes during elections. Politicians who know how to smooth talk their way into people's culture get their vote. It's amazing to note that during election some cultures vote along cultural and religious lines rather than for what the candidate really stands for.

When you examine some of the boroughs of today's multicultural Britain, you will find that people live along cultural lines in cluster groups. We will look carefully at Microstructures and the Macrostructures structures of cultural groupings in multicultural Britain in this study.

Politicians have not been able to define clearly what they mean by the term "multicultural Britain." The phrase is defined by politicians in their own context in a way that will appeal to their audience. To rephrase a contextual mind of a politician will be like saying, "When the frog narrates event from the river-bank to the effect that the crocodile is dead; you have no reason to doubt it."

I remember when our pastor went to America and married a Jewish-American; we were all happy and wished them a happy marriage. Within months of arriving in London, she forced her husband to give up his pastoral duties so that they could migrate to Israel. Within a year of their marriage, the pastor resigned and moved to Israel.

It was evident that she was never happy because she found it very difficult to blend into a society that was dominated by a particular cultural group. She once remarked, "Are we living in India or Pakistan." Did the pastor not make her aware of the community she was going to live in and did the pastor really prepare her for integration into a community she had never lived in?

Surely, America is a multicultural society, but the issue has to do with the community she grew up in. For example, in Britain by merely mentioning of a Borough and anybody can easily tell the dominant race or culture living there. For example, mention of Golders Green and you do not need anybody to tell you the predominant race of people living there.

You walk to China Town and you do not need anybody to tell you what race lives in that area. It is quite obvious that when people travel they do not leave their culture behind rather they go with their culture. This is the reason why when people travel to foreign countries they tend to settle along racial lines. This then poses a problem of integration.

It also creates language barriers which make it difficult for immigrants to learn the language of their adoptive country. Could language barriers be the reason why people of the same race choose to settle in the same area? If this is the case, then the whole idea of multicultural society is defeated. Multi-Cultural Society is supposed be a drive towards integration among people of different races.

The Multi-Cultural system in Britain makes Britain the worst offender in integration. For example, walk into any council office, pick any magazine or forms, and you will find everything in the forms has been translated in Chinese, Indian, Taiwanese, Pakistani and Arab. These are just but a few, the list is endless.

Why would an immigrant want to learn the language of his adopted country in the first place when everything he has to know is available in his native dialect? Even in higher learning institutions like the Open University, it is possible to have examinations translated into the language a candidate knows best. In a country like Germany, it is the reverse: the system is designed to make all immigrants to speak the German language. A Country like Germany encourages immigrants' integration into the community much better. Migrants are encouraged to speak the German language.

When immigrants settle according to their cultural grouping, it is difficult for them to integrate into other communities because they see other cultural grouping as foreign. Such cluster communities build invisible barriers to protect their children against cross-cultural marriage. Children growing in cluster cultures begin to identify themselves with children of their own cultural identity.

Communities like these should be a melting pot for cross-cultural marriage but sad to say, they are not. Whilst the second and third generation may seems to break cultural barriers, they are being held against their will by surviving first generations who appear to have a strong influence over them because of the close bond between them. The reasons for this could be many: they want to maintain a separate cultural identity, the fear of losing control of their children and their way of life and to maintain continuity of customs and traditions.

In a cosmopolitan society, many ethnic groups find it hard to break through when it comes to marriage. They would do anything within their power to stop their children marrying from others cultures or different cultures marrying from their culture. Any attempt to marry into their culture may be resisted. They would rather marry among themselves than give their daughter away to a culture they see as foreign. The problems of cross-cultural marriages have caused so much pain among children born in a multicultural society. Youngsters who fall in love while at college and want to marry after graduation will find themselves being confronted by an aged culture that has no place in a cosmopolitan society.

Some people use a multicultural marriage as a spring board to free themselves from an aging tradition that will not reform itself. For example, women who know their culture enslaves them will take the advantage of being born into a cosmopolitan society as a pretext to break free from a culture that demeans women. Such women marry from different cultures that regard women and men as equals. I know of a West African tribe where the males choose to marry from other cultures because of their system of inheritance. In this culture it is not a man's son that inherits his property, rather his nephew. Cross-cultural shows how complex and profound the issue of this kind of marriage can be.

FUNDAMENTALS OF RELIGIOUS BELIEF

It will be difficult to study cross-cultural marriage and cross-religious marriage without exploring what religion and cultural have in common and what they do not have in common. Religion is intertwined with culture because every culture has a form of worship, this could be a deity, an idol or any form of image they revere. Whatever a culture holds sacred could be what that cultures worships. Therefore, what they reverence forms the religion of the culture.

Let us use the following cultures for the purpose of illustration.

1. **Judaism:** forms the fabric of the Jewish culture, because Jewish culture revolves around their religion. Their way of life, custom and tradition are centred on the religion.
2. **Islam:** forms part of the culture of Arabs. The Arabian culture is centred on the Islamic religion. Their laws and the way they live are dictated by the religion. The religion is the culture and the culture is the religion.
3. **Hinduism:** Religion of India that envelops the Hindu culture and sets out the way Hindus live their lives. The religion is based on caste system, namely 1. Brahmin- the priestly and intellectual class 2. Kshatriyas, the rulers and warriors. 3. Vaisyas, the common agriculturist, and 4. Sudras, the lowest class of the working people. A

culture that is based on system of beliefs and caste systems that binds the religion and the culture together.

DEFINITION OF RELIGION: Religion is a very difficult word to define. Highly educated people, who have studied world religion for years, still find the term hard to describe. In trying to define the term you fine that one definition suits Christianity, but not Islam. One definition defines religion as a belief in the worship of a God or gods. This also entails a personal commitment to a god with worship and devotion. It is a conduct based on obedience to divine command.

1. **COMPLIANCE:** A religion has certain requirements which its followers must comply with in the practice of the religion.
2. **CONFIDENCE:** A religion requires its members to express trust and confidence in the deity. They believe the deity will satisfy the need of life. Those who come to God must believe that HE IS, and that He rewards those that seek Him (Hebrews 11:6).
3. **DEPENDENCE:** A religion requires its adherents to depend on the deity to satisfy some emotional, spiritual, or physical needs.
4. **REVERENCE:** The followers of a religion view the deity with reverence and respect. Thus, their religion is between them and the deity.
5. **TRANSCENDENCE:** Religion directs it followers to a power that goes beyond the human and natural.

THE PURPOSE OF RELIGION: As we come to this critical stage of this chapter, perhaps you may not be a believer of the Christian faith, the Jewish faith or the

Islamic faith. Before we examine critically the views of the three great religions of the Middle East and their views on cross-religious marriage, we have to first, ask the question why each of these religions claim, "There is only one God" and why He alone must be worshipped. But the question we must ask is, if there is indeed only one God, how can we prove His exists? In our attempt to answer the question of the existence of God we must not try to use persuasive ideas that will lead to an empty space.

There is something in the heart of every man that reaches out beyond himself. Even those who claim not to believe in God are often engaged in man's historic quest for an answer to this "heart-hunger." It is not always known to man just what this hunger inside him is. St. Augustine expressed this thought by saying that, "Man is restless until he finds his rest in God."

God, to be truly God, must be more than man can conceive. If He were not, He would not be God. A great preacher, C. H. Spurgeon, once said, "No subject of contemplation will tend more to humble the mind than thoughts of God . . . . It is a subject so vast that all our thoughts are lost in its immensity; so deep, that our pride is drowned in its infinity."

Have you encountered people who claimed they don't believe in the existence of God? It is generally agreed that all people have something they honour that is higher than them. Then the question arises, does God have to seek for man or does man have to seek God? To begin with let's use this illustration. "The followers of some religion compare this search to climbing a mountain that leads to God. They believe that all religions are different roads up to the mountain, and all of them can be accepted, for they all lead to God. You may have heard people say this, but is it true? Man contains a spiritual dimension that can only be satisfied by a source of spiritual life. This dimension can be compared to thirst. Lost in a desert of sin and despair, parched with thirst, man needs water. God provides an oasis. He invites everyone to come to the water to have his soul satisfied. Man is not saved by struggling up the mountain of self-effort, but he is saved by coming to the source of Life. Here one's thirst is satisfied by drinking from the fountain. Here is the end of man's quest.

Jesus once stood in Jerusalem among crowd of people on a Jewish feast day and said, "If anyone is thirsty, let him come to me and drink. Whoever believes in me, as the Scripture has said, streams of living water will flow from within him" (John 7:37-3). See also (Isaiah 55:1).

A friend who happened to be an atheist asked me to prove to him the existence of God. Have you also been asked by someone to prove the existence of God? Or heard people say there is no God and that the ideal of God is man's creation? Philosophers and theologians have examined evidence for God's existence and stated their arguments. While no argument is sufficient in itself, all their arguments present compelling evidence for God's existence. Creation also speaks eloquently of His existence in its harmony and order, and man's moral nature is a reflection of the great moral Designer. The combined evidence provides convincing proof that God exists.

The existence of God is never "proved" in the Bible, it is assumed. God's existence is something you must accept on faith. Neither the Biblical writers nor any of the people to whom they wrote ever questioned whether God exists; so they did not think it was necessary to prove it. If you want to have a relationship with God, you must first believe that He exists. The writer of Genesis makes no attempt to prove that there is a God before he relates the account of Creation. Rather, he assumes the fact of His existence.

The Bible does not attempt to prove God's existence; rather it reveals Him and assumes that there is God. In Psalm 14:1 the Psalmist wrote, the fool says in his heart, "There is no God." The Psalmist may have a valid good reason for making such a statement. The fool's reason could be any of the following. 1. He cannot see God, so how can he prove His existence? 2. He cannot touch God and feel him, so to him there is no God. 3. Can a person belief in what he has not seen, touched and handled and then defend His existence?

A person asking such questions may have difficulties in believing in the existence of God. However, we can infer the existence of the unseen from what we experience. Much the same problem is encountered by scientists as by the Christian apologist. Can we prove the existence of God? The answer is no, but there are indications of His existence.

An atheist friend once asked me to prove the existence of God. To answer his question I quote the French philosopher and physicist Pascal. He said, "In the heart of every man is a God-shaped vacuum which can only be filled by God's son Jesus Christ" In Romans 1:20, the Apostle Paul wrote, "For since the creation of the world, God's invisible qualities, His eternal power and divine nature, have been clearly seen and understood from what has been made."

We recognise that organised systems are designed and caused. It is therefore reasonable to accept the existence of a cause, (Christians believe the first is God). At some point, it becomes less reasonable to doubt than believe. In Psalm 19:1, David wrote, "The heavens declare the glory of God; the skies proclaim the work of His hands." This is enough evidence for a person to believe in God.

The apostle John made a powerful statement in the defence of the existence of God when he said, "That which was from the beginning, which we have heard, which we have seen with our eyes, which we have looked at and our hands touched, this we proclaim concerning the Word of life. The life appeared; we have seen it and testify to it, and we proclaim to you the eternal life, which was with the Father and has appeared to us. We proclaim to you what we have seen and heard, so that you also may have fellowship with us. And our fellowship is with the Father and with the Son, Jesus Christ. We write this to make your joy complete." (1 John 1:1-4).

The apostle Peter wrote these words in defence of God's existence, "We did not follow cleverly invented stories when we told you about the power and coming of our Lord Jesus Christ, but we were eye-witnesses of his majesty." (2 Peter 1:16) These words dispel every cloud of dust surrounding the existence of God and leave evidence of a verdict that doubters cannot disprove.

Those who are reading this book and do not believe in God or his existence should read the following very carefully and see if their unbelief in the existence of God can be challenged or what they are about to read may bring them to the throne of grace where they would acknowledge that there is God and those who seek will find Him and He will reveal Himself to them. The Prophet Jeremiah wrote the following, "You will seek me and find me when you seek me with all your heart." (29:13)

Man's continuous resistance to belief in the existence of God will lead him nowhere. This is what grandfather once said about those who doubt the existence of God, "It is only the one who fetches water at the river side that breaks the pot. Therefore, if the person who fetches the water continuously breaks the pot, the water never gets fetched."

A young man walked into my office and told me the following, "Branford I know you are a Christian and you do preach. I grew up in an atheist family where my parents told me there is no God and we should never belief in God. They told us the idea of God is man's own creation to satisfy his weakness. But I never believed them because something within me kept telling to search for answers myself and that is why I have come to you. I will like to know from you if I was right for not believing my parents. I have a Bible, but the problem is that it is too much for me to read all. Could you show me how I can belief in God and trust in Him?"

One way to explain the existence of God is by using the flow of electrical current as an illustration. No one can see the flow of electrical current, but one can feel its flow by coming in contact with it or stepping on a live cable. Similarly, the Christian God is a Spirit. He cannot be seen, but His presence can be felt by faith through the empowering of the Holy Spirit.

When a person enters a dark room, the normal human instinct is to turn on the light. The light immediately turns the darkness into light. Without the flow of electrical current, the lamps in our homes will not light. Also we cannot turn on the television and other electrical equipment that brings comfort to our homes without the flow of electrical current.

Similarly, without the Word of God, the human race lives in spiritual darkness. The only way to experience the light of God is by reaching out for the lamp of God, which is the Word of God. The Psalmist wrote, "Your word is a lamp to my feet and a light for my path." (Psalm 119:105). Jesus Christ spoke the following words to validate his Testimony, "I am the light of the world. Whoever follows me will never walk in darkness, but will have the light of life" (John 8:12).

We know that when a conductor is moved across a magnetic field, a voltage is induced in the conductor. This principle is called electromagnetic induction, and is defined as inducing voltage in a conductor that moves across a magnetic field. For example, a direct-current generator operates by moving a conductor across a stationary magnetic field to produce voltage and current (North Pole and South Pole). Now, let's use the principles of electromagnetic induction to explain the existence of God;

1. The Bible represents the spiritual North Pole and man represents the South Pole. The two form the spiritual magnetic field.
2. The Holy Spirit is the spiritual conductor which moves between the Word of God and Man. The movement induces a powerful magnetic field which produces Faith of God in man. The faith produced by the Holy Spirit creates the presence of God in the heart and mind of Man and makes him or her believe in the existence of God.
3. As the Holy Spirit moves between the Word of God and Man, it creates a powerful attraction between God and Man. This attraction is spiritual, which induces the love of God that transmits a signal of awareness of God in the person seeking to know God.
4. Without the working of the Holy Spirit no one can know God and come to Him.
5. Faith is the spiritual current produced by the Holy Spirit. Faith alone can make a person feel the presence of God. Faith alone can make a person believe in God. Faith and faith alone can bring a person to the throne of grace. Faith is the

gateway that leads a person seeking to know God and to become aware of God's presence and make him believe and submit to His authority.

6. To summarised this, we have the Bible and man as = North and South Poles. Holy Spirit represents = the conductor. Then the current represents = Faith.

The Holy Spirit induces faith, faith induces the love of God, and then love induces revelation of God. To illustrate this clearly, let's use the battery as an example. The car battery is the heart of the electrical system. It plays its role in the operation of the starter, charging, ignition and accessory.

1. The battery supplies current to the system, and become charged.
2. **The Holy Spirit is the battery:** it serves as the powerhouse that controls and inspires faith and revelation.
3. The generator sends a reverse current to the battery, recharging it.
4. **Revelation is the generator:** It stirs up faith and sends weak faith to the Holy Spirit for spiritual recharging. It is the Holy Spirit alone who can turn weak faith into a strong faith in God.
5. **Faith is the Current:** When faith flows from the Holy Spirit into those who seek God, it energizes faith in God.
6. Current produced by the electrical conductor is carried by the copper cables to our homes or in cars which gives light and operates all our electrical appliances in the car, for example, lights, screen wipers, car radio and C.D player.

7. Similarly, the **Word of God is light.** How does God transfer His light to turn our spiritual darkness into His light?

8. We now know **faith is the current,** but it needs a conductor to carry current to illuminate the light of God in those who seek God.

9. The **Conductor is the Holy Spirit** which enables the Word of God (light) to shine and turn the darkness of those who seek God into His glorious light. Without the Holy Spirit man lives in total spiritual darkness. However, when the Holy Spirit comes into those who diligently seek God it transforms their spiritual darkness into spiritual light. Without the Holy Spirit, it is impossible to be connected to God in order to turn a person's spiritual darkness into spiritual light.

10. God is Spirit and His Spirit inspires faith that will lead a person to believe in Him.

11. The knowledge that enables us to know God as a person, as well as a power, does not come from this world. This knowledge is **divine and supernatural and comes to us only by revelation.** "Man without the Spirit does not accept the things that come from the Spirit of God, for they are foolishness to him, and he cannot understand them, because they are spiritually discerned" (1 Corinthians 2:14). So not only do we need a revelation from God, we also need the help of the Holy Spirit to understand that revelation.

These electrical illustrations show how our homes and vehicles are powered by electrical currents to provide comfort, without which our movement from place to place and development would not be possible.

Similarly without the Bible, the Holy Spirit and Faith it is impossible to know God.

JUDAISM

Judaism is the oldest of the world's three great monotheistic religions and parent of Christianity and Islam. The belief in one God is at the heart of Jewish religion. He is God, who is the Creator and Ruler of all things. He is eternal; He sees everything and knows everything. He speaks to His people through His prophets, and has chosen them as His people to be a light to all mankind.

The word Judaism stems from the word Jew. A Jew was a member of the tribe Judah and of the Jewish nation which existed in Palestine from the sixth century B.C. to the first century A. D. Judah was the name of the ancient Jewish kingdom and originated from the Hebrew word Yehudhi. Judaism is a religion that expresses the beliefs and practice of the Jews, as revealed to Abraham, Moses, and the prophets.

The Jewish people have had the most remarkable history. It is unique in that it brings God's dealing with people directly into view. Besides being called the people of God, the Jewish people have been called Semites, Hebrews, Israelites, and Jews. The ancestry of the Jewish people can be traced back to Abraham who was in the tenth generation of Shem, the eldest son of Noah.

The Bible and Mixed Marriages: The Old Testament prohibits intermarriage with non-Israelites (Deuteronomy 7:3). The author of the book of Kings goes to great lengths to show that Solomon's foreign wives led to his ultimate ruin (1 Kings 11:1-6). Much later, Ezra and Nehemiah even used divorce as a means to reversing the vitiating national consequences of mixed marriages (Ezra 9-10 and Nehemiah 13:23-27). Yet in all of this, the overarching issue is religious faithfulness. When Israel was about to cross the Jordan, the prohibition against mixed marriages focused on the problem of **apostasy.** The LORD warned that Canaanite wives "will turn your sons away from following me to serve other gods, and the LORD'S anger will burn against you and will quickly destroy you" (Deuteronomy 7:4). Solomon became the tragic proof that this warning was necessary.

Nevertheless, there are exceptions. Ruth the Moabitess, for example, became the wife of a prominent Bethlehemite, and she ultimately played an important role in salvation history. She became the great-ancestress of both David and Jesus (Ruth 4:16-22; Matthew 1:5). Intermarriage was not clearly a racial issue in the Old Testament. Rather, the concern was the reality that marriage to someone with radically different commitments and conviction makes it intensely difficult to be faithful to God over the long haul. In fact, the Israelites' experience was that it was nearly impossible to be true to God while being married to a pagan.

This should never become a racial issue. It appeared to be racial in the Old Testament only because each racial group normally consisted of its own nation and religion. But our multicultural, pluralistic environment, interracial marriage is not the issue. Rather, the New Testament is clear that marriage to unbelievers is the issue.

To prevent the Jews from worshipping others gods through intermarriage, God gave them specific instruction not to intermarry with the neighbouring nations around them. The only way to preserve a race and make them serve only one God was by restricting marriage within the same culture. Therefore God gave them the following instructions; **"And when you choose some of their daughters as wife for your sons and those daughters prostitute themselves to their gods, they will lead your sons to do the same" (Exodus 34:16).**

Ezra's reaction to the intermarriage of many of the Jews who had returned from the Exile (Ezra 9:2) might prove instructive. Ezra knew the intermarriage with the Canaanites and other people of Palestine was explicitly condemned. He was also familiar with the prophets' denunciation of the practice.

We know from Scripture that interracial marriage or cross-cultural marriage took place often in the Old Testament. For example, Moses married an Ethiopian woman (Numbers 12:1). Salmon married Rahab, the harlot of Jericho (Matthew 1:5) and Boaz married the Moabite Ruth (Ruth 2:10; 4:13). Nevertheless, God generally cautioned His people against marriage to foreigners because their allegiance to idols and foreign gods would dilute the Israelites allegiance to the one true God.

However, none of the above people angered the LORD for marrying foreign women as Solomon. King Solomon loved and married many foreign women when he knew the LORD had forbidden them from taking foreign women as wives. For the LORD told the Israelites, "You must not intermarry with them, because they will surely turn your hearts after their gods." (1 Kings 11:2). Nevertheless, Solomon held fast to them in love.

We know from the Scriptures the consequences of Solomon's disobedience of the LORD'S commands. "As Solomon grew old, his wives turned his heart after other gods and his was not fully devoted to the LORD his God, as the heart of David his father had been. (1

Kings 11:4). Furthermore, the Scriptures say; "So Solomon did evil in the eyes of the LORD, he did not follow the LORD completely, as David his father had done" (1 Kings 11:6).

The following is what the Scripture says about the consequences of Solomon's disobedience; "The LORD became angry with Solomon because his heart had turned away from the LORD, the God of Israel, who appeared to him twice. Although he had forbidden Solomon to follow other gods, Solomon did not keep the LORD'S command. So the LORD said to Solomon, "Since this is your attitude and you have not kept my covenant and my decrees, which I commanded you, I will most certainly tear the kingdom away from you and give it to one of your subordinates. Nevertheless, for the sake of David your father, I will not do it during your lifetime. I will tear it out of the hand of your son. Yet I will not tear the whole kingdom from him but will give him one tribe for the sake of David my servant and for the sake of Jerusalem, which I have chosen." (1 Kings 11:7-13).

The Bride Price: In Jewish custom, the bride price was the price paid to a bride's family to acknowledge the financial loss created by the woman's marriage. Since a woman became part of her husband's family of origin and was impoverished by her marriage. The bride price repaid at least a token of the family's loss of a productive worker. It was often a gift of substantial value.

Women in the ancient world: The record of Leah and Rachel stands out among the writings and women as little more than property. Furthermore, the men who recorded the literature of those times tended to overlook the presence and significance of their female counterparts.

CONCUBINES: Leah and Rachel, the wives of Jacob, used their maids to compete with each other for their husband's favour by having them bear his children (Genesis 30:3-13). Thus, the maids Zilpah and Bilhah became secondary wives or "concubines" to Jacob. The practice of "marrying" concubines as a form of polygamy was known throughout the ancient Middle East.

A concubine was usually a female slave with whom the leading male of the family was free to have sexual relations. She was not considered an equal to his "full" wife (or wives), and she could not be sold if the man lost interest in her. However, rights varied from culture to culture. One of the main reasons for keeping a concubine was to give birth to children, particularly a son and therefore an heir. See Genesis Chapter 16 and Judges Chapter 11.

Hagar: Married cross-culturally to a husband who probably did not share her faith, she reared a son who later served as a leader in the early Church.

INTERMARRIAGE: Some segments of the modern-day Church around the world, especially those in the inner cities and developing countries, struggle with issues related to intermarriage between races and different ethnic groups. For these believers, Ezra's reaction to the intermarriages of many of the Jews who had returned from the Exile (Ezra 9:2) might prove instructive.

AN INTERRACIAL MARRIAGE: The marriage that was celebrated in the Song of Solomon appears to have been a match between two members of different ethnic groups. The groom, presumably Solomon, is described as "white and ruddy" (Songs 5:10), while the bride is "dark" like the black tent of Kedar (see "A Dark-Skinned Bride" at Song 1:5-6). If these description indicate skin colour, then Solomon was evidently married a woman from different ethnic background.

Marrying across ethnic and racial lines was not uncommon in the ancient world (for example, Numbers 12:1; Ruth 1:4; 1 King 11:1). Today, however, it poses a problem for some. Yet it is important to note that whatever reasons people may have for opposing intermarriage or cross-cultural marriage, the Bible neither condemns them nor prohibits them (see Deut. 7:1-4, 23:3). These prohibitions were not based on ethnicity but had to do with religion, morality, and geopolitical considerations.

God created a diversity of races on the earth. Differences in background and skin colour may be hard for people to accept, but not for God. He Himself reaches out to all the peoples of the world (see Matthew 28:19), so it is not surprising that His Word may celebrate a marriage between two people from different ethnic groups.

If God created man, both male and female, in His own image, then it follows that the male and female are equal before Him. Yet in many cultures even today, vast inequalities exist between men and women. Women are often treated unfairly. For example, in modern society, working women often do not enjoy the same job opportunities as men even if they are equally qualified; or if they do the same job as men, their pay is lower than the man's pay.

Women in the Jewish culture of Jesus' day were generally treated rather badly. Marriages were arranged by parents and a girl would be married at the age of 13 or 14. Then she would become the property of her husband. In the temple, she could only worship in the outer court especially reserved for women. Her husband could divorce her for any reason; for example, if she happened to burn his food, he could divorce her. The low status of women is clearly revealed in one of the daily prayers of Jewish men: "Blessed is God who has not made me a woman!"

There is nothing in Scripture to suggest that the female has received less of the image of God than the male. Rather, we learn from the New Testament that Christ's work of restoring the image of God in man gives to all men and women the same measure of dignity. Jesus showed a very different attitude toward women than that of the Jewish men of His day. He treated them with a dignity that was unknown among Jewish at that time.

For example, He did not despise the woman who had lived a sinful life when she came to see Him, anointed Him with perfume, and wiped His feet with her hair. Rather, He spoke a word of comfort to her and forgave her sins. By contrast, the Pharisee showed deep contempt for her (Luke 7: 36-50). Furthermore, Jesus did not condone divorce for any reason except for "marital unfaithfulness" (Matthew 5: 31-32). Finally, Jesus demonstrated by His actions that He did not look upon women as men's property but as their partners in marriage.

This does mean that there are no distinctions between male and female. As a matter of fact, the Bible clearly recognizes that there are differences in functions. The apostle taught that "the husband is the head of the wife as Christ is the head of the Church, his body," and that "as the Church submits to Christ, so the wives should submit to their husband in everything" (Ephesians 5:23-24). This headship of the husband carries with it responsibility of loving the wife. (Ephesians 5:25-28).

ISLAM

Islam is a religious movement founded by the prophet Muhammad in the early part of the seventh century A.D. The word Islam comes from the Arabic word Salam, meaning "surrender, submission, peace, and commitment." Islam is faith in Allah which means "The God." It combines the Arabic article al ("the") with the Arabic word Illah, meaning "God." Hence, Islam means the "perfect peace that comes from total surrender to Allah."

Islam emphasis the success of its beliefs and is therefore a militant missionary religion. The faithful have inscribe in front of every Mosque, impressively, the following words, **"There is no God but Allah; Muhammad is His prophet."**

Like Christianity, Islam, has its roots in Judaism, except that it has no place for the idea of the Son of God. Islam recognises great men like Noah, Abraham, Jesus and Muhammad as prophets, called and chosen by God, but still ordinary men.

In the Muslim view of religion, the law or Shari' a, meaning "Well-known path," is most important. While the Quran speaks of God's compassion and mercy on repentant sinners, Islam is more concerned with obedience than with forgiveness. Under the Islamic Law, it is the duty of the faithful to accept what the prophet said without asking how or why. Hence, any inquiry into a theology of Islam, such a Christians have, is wrong and probably heretical. For this reason, Islamic scholars have given themselves much to the study of the law or Shari 'a

Statues of women: Before Muhammad, women had very low social status in Arabia. They were considered slaves or property of the father, husband or elder brother. They could be divorced by a husband whenever he desired. Sometimes female babies were killed. Muhammad raised the statues of women to a large extent, although not to the equality of men.

Muhammad allowed polygamy and was married to a number of women himself, some of whom were widows of Muslims killed in battle. However, he limited the number of wives of Muslims to four, provided they could afford them.

In Islam, Muslim women are forbidden to marry non-Muslims. The reason for this is that because in marriage women are to submit to their husbands, the possibility of them being converted to the faith of the person they are married to is much greater. They believe women who are married to other men of different faith may not be able to raise the children in the Muslim faith.

In some cases, Muslim women who disobey the religion and their parents and marry from outside Islam are known to face sudden death. Those who think this is not possible better read the following story. Hannah was a school friend. She was a Muslim girl whose father was the chief Imam of our town. In our final year, her best friend who was a Christian invited her to an Easter convention. At the convention she gave her life to Christ and publicly denounced her Islamic faith.

After graduating she went home thinking she could evade detection by hiding her new found faith in Christ. She started giving excuses for skipping Friday prayers, then the family noticed she was out of the house every Sunday morning and came home late. The family hired a private detective to follow her and find out where she had been going. One Sunday morning, the private detective followed her to the local Baptist Church, and then reported back to the family. Then, the following Sunday, just as she was getting ready to go to Church, she was confronted by the grim faces of her parents and siblings. When she realised she had been found out, she confessed her faith in Christ.

By this statement she had pronounced her own death. She was given five minutes to denounce her faith in Christ and revert back to the Islamic faith. Then the clock started ticking. When the clock stopped at the time given, her father asked her, "Have you arrive at a decision?" She said, "Yes I stand with Christ."

At this her father told her brothers; "You know what to do." Well here there is no difference between killing and instructing others to kill. It's exactly the same thing, or even worse. Being alive today was a lucky escape for her. Because she was her father's favourite daughter, she was spared the death sentence.

She was dragged outside and stripped completely naked and told and go to the "People of the book." However through the most marvellous divine intervention, a woman appeared from nowhere with a new set of clothes and shoes for her. The woman quickly used a cloth to cover her, and then stood next to her while she dressed. The strange woman hugged her and smiled and then disappeared. That was the last time Hannah ever saw the woman.

At the Church the pastor put her up with a family who took good care of her. After a year in the church, the pastor married Hannah in a colourful wedding to the delight and joy of the congregation. After six years of marriage they were blessed with two boys and two girls. The thought of having been disowned by her parents created a void in her life because she felt part of her was missing. She was the darling of the family and her father adored her very much. Hannah was the pride and joy of her father and this made her depressed.

When she heard her father was dying she managed to make contact with her family through family friends. She finally succeeded in re-establishing ties with her parents at the expense of her faith in Christ. Sometimes it is very difficult to break bonds. As a child growing up, she became naturally attached to her father. Her birth coincided with a financial fortune in the family. She was seen as the girl who turned the family from rags to riches.

The apostle Peter sounds a warning in his second book that reads, "If they have escaped the corruption of the world by knowing our Lord and Saviour Jesus Christ and are again entangled in it and overcome, they are worse off at the end than they were at the beginning. It would have been better for them not to have known the way of righteousness, than to have known it and then turn their back to the sacred command that was passed on to them. Of them the proverbs are true: "A dog returns to its vomit," and, "A sow that is washed goes back to her wallowing in the mud" (2 Peter 2:20-22).

"As a dog returns to its vomit." So Hannah returned to her vomit by the sudden return to her family. She was so overwhelmed by the reunion that she placed the love of her parents above her Salvation and the love for her husband and children. Her spiritual life moved from being hot to cold. There is nothing wrong with a Christian nursing her unbelieving sick father; it even offers such a person an opportunity of leading his or her father to faith in Jesus Christ. But for a Christian to allow the light of Christ in her to be turned to darkness by another faith raises questions.

Grandfather once said, "The way we worship reveals the God we are worshipping. And they way we live our life reveals the kind of God we worship." By spending more time at the family home nursing her father came with its consequences. Months of staying in the family house nursing her sick father led to breakdown in fellowship with Christ and other believers. Besides, months of lack of effective fellowship, prayer and Bible study seriously affected her spiritual life.

Whilst Hannah was busy nursing her sick father, her husband was diagnosed with diabetes. By the time the diabetes was discovered it had affected his eyesight. Within months of being diagnosed he was blind. Hannah, unable to cope with a sick father and blind husband, divorced her husband and moved in permanently with her parents. Disease and suffering can bring families together, but they can also tear families apart. This is often the case of those whose problems are largely the result of their own choices, especially choices that have gone against what the family would have wanted. Grandmother once said, *"She saw integrity as the currency of the Christian marriage and its survival depended on prayer."*

There are no such restrictions placed on Muslim men. Muslim men are allowed to marry from any faith or culture with the authority as the head of the family to covert both the wife who is of different faith and the children to Islam. In Islam, children are the property of the father because they inherit the father's religion.

It the duty of every Muslim husband to raise their children in Islamic faith. Failure would mean he has failed in his duty as a Muslim and as head of the family. Accordingly, in Islam the children are bound to follow their parent's religion. Children born in the Muslim faith have no option of opting out of their parent's religion. In Islam, opting out of parent's religious beliefs comes with a dire consequence.

Muhammad taught his followers not to tolerate pagans. The concept of pagan in Islam refers to a non-Muslim. Why then are Muslim men allowed to marry non-Muslim women, when there was a clear guideline by Muhammad concerning these issues? Is this a question of hypocrisy or disregard of what their sacred book stands for?

It will interest to know that Muhammad himself was married to different women, one of whom was a Jewess and a Christian. There will always be a question surrounding these teachings and its contradiction; however, we must give honour to whom honour is due. Muhammad provided the Arabic people with a sacred book that made them aware of the majesty and power of one true God.

In a multicultural Society, we regularly hear from the television news and read in newspapers about Muslim fathers who have absconded with children never to be seen again. The following reasons may hold keys to unlock the minds of these Muslim fathers. 1. Mothers object to their children being educated in religious fanatic schools. 2. Brain washing of their children's mind to a faith they see as foreign. 3. Differences in religious opinions, which the husband who is the final authority in the home, will not compromise on. 4. Arranged marriages for their daughters to Muslim men.

This is a wake up call for women of different faiths or women without faith to think very carefully before making their decision to be involved in a marriage in which their spouse's religion is only interested in control of the children. This means to control and raise the children in the Islamic faith. A religion that sees men as a dominant authority to control the family should be giving a thoughtful consideration to before making a decision.

In multicultural society cross-cultural marriage is unavoidable because the opposite sex of different cultures and faith can be attracted to each other sexually. Hence, we are faced with dilemma of sons and daughters of different faiths and cultures who are in love and want to marry. The only obstacle that stands in their way is outdated cultures that regard such marriages as unacceptable; and religious beliefs with well founded reasons to regard such marriages as unacceptable.

For the perseverance of the Islamic faith, Muslims may be right to protect to their women against cross-religious marriage in order to keep, the religion undiluted and preserve its purity from a multi-cultural society. Islam has a good case in preventing their women from marrying men from different faith because of their belief that the man being the head of the family is also the final authority in the home.

The Islamic view of a multicultural society is to coexist with other faith and cultures without being assimilated into them. Muslim believes that in a multicultural society having a separate identity keeps them and their religion separate. They see multicultural society as a system that wants to absorb them into one culture.

Islam believes in segregation within a Multi-cultural society rather than integration because of the fear of being absorbed into a social structure that is not steered towards their beliefs. Hence, in Multi-cultural Britain we are faced with self-segregation with the view of turning Britain into an Islamic nation.

With the exception of Christianity, the other two great religions of the Middle East have erected an unbreakable religious barrier around them which is difficult to pull down. The scenario here is that you have either to be like them or stay out of their limelight.

To be like them is to accept their faith and the teaching of the Koran.

CHRISTIANITY

Christianity is a religion that has roots in Judaism and yet has extended its branches far beyond those borders; Christianity spans many cultures and nations and is by far the largest faith in the world. Like Judaism and Islam, Christianity originated from the Middle East. The founder of this faith was a man of low social standing.

During his life, he was unknown outside the corners of the Roman Empire where he lived and died. He never owned a home or had a family of His own. Yet He spoke extensively about marriage and used marriage to illustrate the Kingdom of God. He had few earthly possessions and little money yet He spoke about the dangers of covetousness.

He gave hope and life to those he touched. He built no temple and wrote no book. Nevertheless, He was the inspiration behind the Scriptures, besides; the whole of the New Testament is centred on His work of redemption. He did no wrong, broke no law, yet he died on a criminal's cross, and was buried in a borrowed tomb. (People and their belief By Paul Wright).

The statement **"Upon this rock I will build my church is evident that Jesus Christ is the foundation of the church rather than the founder** (Matthew 16:18) because of the use of the future tense. The accounts of Luke in Acts 1:1 indicates that the founding and spread of Christianity by the apostles was the under the **leadership of the Holy Spirit.** From this we can clearly say the Jesus Christ is the **foundation of the Church and the Holy Spirit if the founder of the Church.**

The Bible: the **Infallible Word-** The word infallible means "incapable of deceiving or making a mistake." word of God means, **"God's word is nondeceptive and unfailing." It does not deceive or mislead, for it is the utterance of God "who does not lie" (Titus 1:2).**

Scripture stands above everything else and judges it. There is no higher authority for the Christian than God's Word. The Bible is sola Scriptura, which means that it alone is the Word of God and it is fully adequate to communicate God's will to man.

1. Since God is the Creator, there can be no ultimate conflict between knowledge from special revelation (what the Bible says) and creation (also known as "general revelation"; what nature says).

2. "The Bible is the Word of God addressed to the heart of man" (Greidanus 1982, 140). Hence sincere submissions to the Lord who speaks through the Scriptures and is revealed in them enable us to see reality, however imperfectly, from God's perspective, the only proper perspective.

3. The Bible is a historical book written first to a particular people in their culture at a certain time, answering their questions and meeting their needs. Thus the Biblical message to us today cannot be understood properly without understanding its historical and cultural context.

4. The Bible was written in non-scientific, everyday language that sometimes used (or assumed) commonly held "scientific" concepts of that time but which we now know to be false. But this

does not mean that the Bible teaches those concepts.

5. Biblical passages must be understood in the author's intention or meaning, and in the light of the totality of the Biblical revelation. It is especially important to remember that obscure or unclear Biblical passages are to be interpreted in light of clearer, more unequivocal passages, and deference must be given to the cumulative weight of many passages over one seemingly clear text if there is apparent conflict.

The Christian marriage is unique and different from all other marriages. Its uniqueness has to do with the beauty of Christ in both the husband and wife. The beauty of the Christian marriage is that the nature of husband and wife is refined by the blood of Jesus Christ. The Christian marriage is designed by God to be evangelistic in its approach, this is why the nature of both spouse has to be refined by the cleansing blood of Jesus Christ.

The Christian marriage is one of God's means of reaching out to heal broken marriages; the Christian marriage is a counselling marriage. When things are going wrong in others' marriages, it is the Christian marriage that becomes a means through which God reaches out to mend and restore peace in the marriage of unbelievers. If there is any marriage the world can look up to for its purity then it is the Christian marriage, because in the Christian marriage we see the beauty of Jesus Christ. When the Christian marriage is submitted to the Lordship and kingship of Christ then it becomes refined by the Blood of Jesus Christ. When a marriage is refined by the Blood of Christ, the marriage never grows cold.

Marriage built on Jesus Christ has all the nutrients it requires to blossom. Such Christian marriages are visibly blossomed because of Christ from whom they derive their nourishment. For the Christian marriage to survive in this present age will involving four things, these are:

1. The Word of God
2. The power of prayer
3. Seeking each other's highest interest
4. Biblical principles

The Christian marriage is meant to grow from strength to strength because of the beauty of Christ. When Christian marriages are not working then it means they have ignored Biblical principles of marriage. If married Christians live their lives as the Scriptures commands then there is no reason why the marriage cannot hold together. However, if we refuse to live the Christian marriage on Biblical principles as the Scriptures command, then we have ourselves to be blamed.

Status of women: Ephesians 5:22-23, "Wives submit to your husbands, as to the Lord. For the husband is the head of the wife, as Christ is the head of the Church; and He is the Saviour of the body." Here Christ calls His children to a lifestyle of submission. **SUBMISSION + RESPONSIBILITY = LOVE.**

It must be pointed out clearly that submission in this content has nothing to do with status (one person being above another or the husband being above the wife), rather with role and function. Submission is identifying the role, responsibility, or function of the other person in my life and then allowing him to fulfil that function. That is allowing the person to be what God intends him to be.

Peter lists the following advice to Christian husband and wives. If you study verses 1 to 7 of chapter 3 in his first epistle, you note the following:

1. **Wives:** (a) Submissive (b) good behaviour (c) purity (d) reverence (e) outward appearance (f) inner self (g) gentle (h) quiet spirit (i) what is right and (k) fear.
2. **Husbands:** (a) considerate (b) respect (c) weaker partner (d) gracious gift and (e) hindrance to prayer. When there is discord in marriage, prayers are hindered. "**The sights of the injured wife come between the husband's prayers and God's hearing." (Bigg)** Also it is very difficult for a couple to pray together when something is disrupting their fellowship. You will need to study these verses very carefully over and over until you fully understand what the Holy Spirit is saying to all Christian husbands and wives.

Reverence: "When they see the purity and reverence of your lives" (3:2). What does Peter mean by this? George Muller told a story of a wealthy German whose wife was a committed Christian. This man was a heavy drinker, spending late nights in the pub. She would send the servants to bed, stay up till he returned, welcome him and never complain. Sometimes she would undress him and put him to bed. One night in the pub, he told his friends, "I go home and my wife will be sitting down waiting for me. As soon as she sees me she will come to the door and give us a royal welcome, and even make supper for us, if I ask her. They were sceptical at first, but decided to follow him home to see for themselves. To their amazement she came to the door to welcome them courteously and willingly agreed to make supper for them without the slightest sign of

169

resentment. After serving them, she went to her room. As soon as she had left, one of the men began to condemn the husband. "What kind of man are you to treat such a good woman so miserably?" Then the accuser without finishing his supper left the house. Then one by one they all left for their homes without eating the meal. Within half an hour, the husband became deeply convicted of his wickedness, and especially of his heartless treatment of his lovely wife. He went to his wife's room, asked her to pray for him, repented of his sins and surrendered to Christ. From that time on, he became a devoted disciple of the Lord Jesus. Won without a word!

Marriage is a lifelong commitment; for this reason Christians should be very careful before taking the first step into marriage. Although love is the prerequisite for marriage, we should not be blinded by it and sacrifice our Christian faith for the sake of love. The joy of the Christian marriage comes only by marrying according to God's will. The Christian should never negotiate his or her Salvation on the basis of marriage. What do we mean by this statement? It simply means marrying someone from a different faith just because you love him or her.

Most Christian marriages breakdown for the reason they marry. Christians who cannot find the kind person they are looking for in the church and turn to seek for bride or groom outside the community of believers are not only putting themselves in an unhappy marriage but their Salvation is at stake. Cross-religious marriage is the darkest and the most dangerous path for Christians to follow. Cross-religious marriage desecrates the spirit of the Christian marriage and a Christian who dares such a marriage will find the name **Ichabod** written in front of their marital home. **"The glory of God has departed from the marriage."**

The following is a story is about a daughter of a retired Scottish Presbyterian minister who met a young Hindu medical student while they were studying at university. Three years after graduation they married in a Hindu temple. Ten years after marriage they were blessed with a son and two daughters. They are a happy couple and have made cross-cultural marriage the envy of those who oppose marriage between two cultures. On the other hand, it was a deadly mission for this young Christian who thought she could easily flout God's commandments by picking and choosing what suited her and rejecting what she saw as a stumbling block to her happiness. Although their marriage is a very wonderful marriage with affection for each other, nevertheless, this young Christian woman has grown very cold to the things of God. Fellowship with Christians no longer appeals to her. Her marriage is her priority and not fellowship with God.

Her prayer life is virtually dead because of lack of communication between her and Christ. In the worldly sense she was very happy, but spiritually there was an empty void. Spiritual death occurs the moment fellowship with Christ stops. This is what happens to Christians who deliberately put God the Father, God the Son and God the Holy Spirit out of their marital homes. Christians who think they can go to bed with the Bible on the right side of their bed and other religious books on the left side better think carefully about the repercussions.

I have seen countless Christians who have gone outside the community of believers and brought a non-Christian into the Church hoping they could be converted to the Christian faith, so that they could marry them. Christians like these are already living an immoral life. To think you can bring someone of a different faith into the church to convert the person for the purpose of marriage is like thinking you can make an empty sack stand upright.

When Christian marriage ends in divorce, it brings shame to the Christian faith and the Christian marriage. It affects the cause of God's plan for the institution of marriage which is one of the channels of reaching the unsaved with the message of salvation. When believers are rebuked by non-believers for the way they conduct their marriage it brings shame upon God's people and robs them of opportunity and privilege of being effective witnesses for Christ. When a Christian marriage ends in divorce, it denies the unbelievers opportunity of seeing the beauty of Christ in the Christian marriage. God's power and grace can be experienced through the Christian marriage.

It is the responsibility of married Christians to set a good example by doing what is right in their marriage. Married Christians must demonstrate integrity, self-control and the soundness of our speech so that they cannot be condemned by unbelieving world who are watching us. In this way those who oppose the Christian faith become ashamed because they have nothing negative to say about the marriage.

In 1 Corinthians chapter 7, Paul states the Principles of divorce: Paul carries the teachings of Jesus on divorce over into a new context, but makes the same application: no divorce for believers. I think that still holds, but not because it is the law. It relates more to a basic understanding of the church as God's temple, His new humanity, His new people's Spirit. Two believers, who are brothers and sisters in Christ, should be seeking to love one another as Christ loved them. Two Christians who are brother and sister blessed by God in a holy matrimony are commissioned by God to keep that bond of the Christian marriage together until death separates them. Christians who break the bond of holy matrimony have absolutely nothing to gain. Their action only brings shame to the very faith in Christ they profess.

It is obvious that many young Christians are getting into cross-religious marriages these days without understanding this type of marriage. Their perceptions of marriage are all wrong. All they think about is sex and having children. They have not the slightest idea how to raise children in cross-religious marriage. This issue is made more complex by marrying into a culture of where they have little or no knowledge.

It is the responsibility of Christian parents to do all they can to help their children make a good marriage, although the manner of choosing a spouse these days places more responsibility on the person who is marrying than the generation before it. In a world where a daughter or son can walk into a Church and walk out with a husband or wife, and parents have nothing to say or do about it is why we have broken marriages and unhealthy family relationships within Christendom.

CROSS-RELIGIOUS MARRIAGE

"These things happened to them as examples and were written down as warning for us, on whom the fulfilment of the ages has come." (1 Corinthians 10:22).

Commercial aircraft carry two flight-data called "black boxes." One logs the performance and condition of the aircraft in flight, and the other records the conversation of the crew with air-traffic controllers on the ground. These boxes are insulated to protect against extreme temperatures and are fitted with underwater located beacons that emit sounds to the surface. After a plane crash, these boxes are retrieved and the data carefully analysed to determine the cause of the crash. Air safety experts want to learn from past mistakes, among other things, so they won't be repeated.

As Christians we too should look at mistake from the past and learn from them when it comes to marriage. God in His own wisdom did not conceal anything from us and allowed everything be written in the Scriptures. He did this for our own good so that we do not repeat the same mistake His prophets, leaders and kings did to bring shame to His Holy name. Just as God exposed them for their disobedience so will He expose us if we follow the same line of disobedience.

You will find scattered throughout this chapter ten serious warnings. They are like high way sign warning of a washed-out bridge or floodwater that makes the road ahead impassable. Ignoring the warning can lead to disaster, but every warning written in this book have exhortation about what to do to avoid the danger. Study this chapter very carefully and take not of the warnings and what to do to avert the dangers. You must pay close attention to what has been said in this book so that you don't drift away from the warning the Scripture gives so that you don't fall into a marriage that will bring you misery and end in divorce. For those who simply ignore the warnings on cross-religious marriage spoken by the LORD and Paul as stated in the Scriptures are bound to face marriage problems.

Without question, cultural circumstances play part in people's religious beliefs. A Hindu background would tend to predispose a person towards Hinduism, a Christian background towards Christianity, and so forth. Similarly, when it comes to marriage a true Christian is drawn like a magnet towards a relationship with of the opposite sex who is also a Christian. But can social conditioning alone explain why people believe and behave as they do? After all, a Christian upbringing is no guarantee that a Christian would not abandon his or her religious beliefs and marry someone of a different faith. On the other hand, countless Christians who have not been exposed to the word of God either through laziness in studying the Scriptures or if he of she is not from a Bible-teaching Church could wonder away and marry someone from another faith.

What is the Scripture's view about cross-cultural marriage? To begin with, we need to distinguish the difference between **Cross-Cultural Marriage and Cross-Religious Marriage.** Cross-cultural marriage: This is where two people from different cultures fall in love with each other and decides to live together as husband and wife. For example, a German man marrying a Chinese woman or a Turkish woman married to an English man.

Cross-religious marriage has to do with two people from different religious faiths that fall in love and decide to live together as a husband and wife. The Scripture does not place a ban on cross-cultural marriage, rather places a ban on cross-religious marriage. Cross-religious marriage amounts to idolatry. A cross-religious marriage is one of the most effective channels Satan uses to draw the believer from the Saving grace of our Lord Jesus Christ. Also cross-religious marriage can draw the Christian into idol worshiping. This is the reason God forbade His chosen people from inter-marriage.

To cross religious boundaries to marry a man or woman you love is like sitting at a table with the devil to negotiate your Salvation. When it comes to cross-religious marriage, the Scriptures have nothing to negotiate with a Christian who is bent on disobeying what the Scriptures say is right. The fact is that cross-religious marriage is out of bounds to the Christian.

Therefore, a person who has professed faith in Christ must live his or her life in obedience to the teachings of Christ. There is no point professing your faith in Christ and living your life independently of Christ. A Christian who gets entangled in cross-religious marriage is like an immature swimmer who jumps into the sea to rescue a drowning person after a few hours of swimming lessons.

This brings back a story I read from local news paper about a man who took his family for holiday for the first time. As the family were enjoying their first day at the beach, his son wandered away and found himself walking along a stairway cut into a rocks on the small remote island. As the father watched him, he was swept out to sea by a large wave. Human instinct moved a loving and caring father to jump into the sea to save his son, when he knew he had never leaned how to swim. By leaping into the sea to rescue his son, he was swept away by the wave. Christians going into cross-religious marriage marriages can be like this father.

This is a principle worth keeping in mind. Today as Church leaders try to help believers wrestle with issues of intermarriage, we should be mindful of the pitfall in cross-religious marriage. The main question to consider is not of ethnicity, but faith in Jesus Christ. Is the person you want to marry a Christian? How can you prove that the person you are marrying is a Christian? What things should the Christian look for when it comes to cross-religious marriage? When marriage compromises your faith in Christ, then it is not worth it.

In the Old Testament God forbid the marriage between Jews and non Jews. The reasons were His covenant relationship with them. Today that bond has not changed. Christians who flout this command will find they are drifting from the Christian faith to their spouse's faith. The danger here is that they will find themselves trapped in a marriage that takes Jesus Christ out of the marriage and replace Him with another religious founder.

The issue of cross-religious marriage is clearly stated in Scriptures without any ambiguities. In 2 Corinthians 6:14-17, the apostle Paul writes', "Do not be yoked together with unbelievers. For what do righteousness and unrighteousness have in common? Or what fellowship can light have with darkness? What harmony is there between Christ and Belial? What does a believer have in common with an unbeliever? What agreement is there between the temple of God and idols? For we are the temple of the living God. As God has said; "I will live with them and walk among them, and I will be their God, and they will be my people". "Therefore come out from them and be separated" says the Lord.

The verse above could be referred to a Christian marrying an unbeliever. Marriages that are not built on the foundation of Jesus Christ are bound to fail. A Christian cannot marry someone of different religious faith if he wants to obey the Word of God. However, in cases where the believer is already married to an unbeliever this verse does not justify separation or divorce. God's will in such a case is that the marital relationship should be maintained with a view to the eventual Salvation of the unsaved member.

For the Christian, marrying a person of different religious faith spells disaster for the marriage because it would be difficult for husband and wife to worship a different God without some form of compromise. Besides, the Scripture forbids Christians to compromise their faith for a cause that will lead them to lose their Salvation. Christians who marry from other religious faiths are not really Christians but liberal Christians. Liberal Christians are the reason Christian marriages are given a bad name.

The divorce stigma associated with most Christian marriages is the result of marriages between liberal Christians. In the Church, it is sometimes very difficult to know who a liberal Christian is. This makes it more difficult when it comes to choosing a future spouse. When wolves are dressed in sheep skin it posses a dilemma for unsuspecting Christians. Even some pastors are unable to sieve through the grain and separate the grain from the chaff. To unmask the wolves from the sheep takes the spirit of discernment and not many Christians have this gift.

The most disturbing thing is that some Pentecostal pastors would marry any one who walks into their Church and picks a bride or bridegroom. No questions asked as to the level of commitment, how they met and decided to live together as husband and wife, are both of them ready for marriage, and have they prayed and heard God's will for them?

The Christian intending to marry a man or woman of different religious faith should answer the following questions, "How can a Christian who is faithful to Christ be married to a man or woman who does not accept or recognized Christ as the Son of God? Does the Scripture allow Christians to go into a marital union with people of other faith? Can Christians live in a matrimonial home where one of them does not acknowledge the Lordship and the kingship of Jesus Christ? Is it possible for a Christian to be married to a person who does not accept Christ as the only way to Salvation? Can a Christian live in such a marriage and pray without the prayer being hindered?

If the devil knocks on your door and proposes a business deal and you think doing business with him will give him access to your children then shut the door before him. You have nothing to lose shutting the door in front of the devil. What you should never do is to give the devil a precondition for a business transaction because he will gladly accept the conditions, then use it as a pretext to gain access to your home. Your daughter or son will be of interest to him more than the business.

The devil is notorious for breaking promises and should never be trusted. He is like a pig that goes back to wallow in the muddy waters after a good wash or dog that goes back to its vomit after it has been well fed. If you do not want to dine with the devil, do not give him an open invitation to your home. Doing business with the devil is a tragic mistake that has caused so much pain in the lives of people who thought they could keep him in check. The devil is a crooked business man and a schemer and should never be given an audience. I am sure nobody would want to go into a business venture with a dishonest person like the devil.

179

Satan is a con man and that is who he really is. Doing business with him will lead you to surrender your birthright to him.

The devil is a cleaver and a deceiving spirit who cunningly causes the strongest to fall into the temptation of marrying his children. It is only by being alert and sensitive to the Holy Spirit and making God's warnings our daily concern that we can resist the devil. In fact we are capable of turning our testimony of Jesus Christ into a sham when we walk away from His counsel for the sake of satisfying our desires. Only God's grace and power can keep us from falling and pick us up from where we have fallen.

If the devil's son knocks on your door and asks for your daughter's hand in marriage, say nothing and slam the door in front of him. Similarly, if your son comes home with the devil's daughter, tell him the woman he has brought will never make a good wife for him because she is a product of darkness while he is of the product of light. It is the responsibility of every Christian parent to make their children understand that a child of God who walks from light into darkness to marry a woman of his choice would be severing fellowship with Jesus Christ.

Grandmother once said, "Love can divide families." However, this should never be used as a pretext for Christian parents to give their consent to their children marrying from other religions. The following Scriptural verse is worth reading now: "And do not grieve the Holy Spirit with whom you have been sealed for the day of redemption" (Ephesians 4:30).

I know of a young man who is the managing director of his father's business. Unknown to his parents he had been dating a young Muslim woman he met at a friend's birth day party. Then one day he foolishly walked into his parent's home with the woman and introduced her as his fiancée. This young man underestimated the power of the Holy Spirit in his father. When a Christian lives as if he is possessed by the Holy Spirit the devil stays away from him. This is what the son should have seen in his father. The father looked intensely at his son and said, "This family is a Christian family. If you have forgotten who you are in Christ we have not forgotten who we are in Christ. You have to choose between the family and its business or walk out with your fiancée and be disinherited." Tragically, he walked out with his fiancée from light into a dark domain. Christians who choose to walk into hell because they are attracted and tempted by what the devil offers them will only have themselves to be blamed.

The temptation for our children to go behind the hidden door of secrecy that God has shut in front of them for their own selfish interest will lead them to do things that will mar their integrity and eventually lead them into marriage that will dishonour God. Only God's grace and power can stop us from such unholy marriages.

If you marry the devil's daughter, he becomes your father in-law. Similarly, if you give your daughter's hand in marriage to the devil's son, Satan and his demons will become a regular guest in your home. They will not need any permission from you before they come to your home. They will come whenever they choose and leave whenever they want to. If you make your marital home comfortable for the devil he will never leave. Never allow the devil a resting place in your matrimonial home.

When you allow the devil into your home, he will place his seal of ownership on your doorpost as a mark of joint ownership. These seal is a spiritual seal that guarantees Satan's demons the right to claim ownership of the marriage. These are the reasons why the divorce rate among the Christian community is very high. There is a Ghanaian proverb which, when interpreted, reads, **"When you are going into marriage, ask."** The proverb sums up the whole of divorce plight that has ravaged the Institution of Marriage while pastors have fruitlessly searched for answers.

Satan, because of his hatred of Christianity and the Christian marriage, has become the architect of cross-religious marriage. He will always coax his client to believe that there is nothing morally or spiritually harmful in cross-religious marriage as long as love plays the central role in the marriage. He is the one who benefits from such marriage. If the reasons for your marriage benefit the devil more than Christ, then there is something seriously wrong with your marriage. Christians who think they can marry their childhood sweetheart who is not a Christian better think of the consequences before committing themselves to such a marriage.

Satan is the one to be blame for all the suffering and failed Christian marriages. He is the supreme master of all the evil spirits that are at war against Christian marriages. All the trouble Christians faced in the marriages are caused by him. Since being thrown out of heaven, he fights against God by attacking all the institution ordained by God which includes Christian marriages. The good news is that the more Satan tries to cause havoc in Christian marriage the more other Christian tries to resist him.

Cross-cultural marriages can be good but they come with certain problems. Some of these problems are spiritual while, others can be physical problems. For the Christian, the need to unearth the very fabric of your fiancée's culture before committing yourself is very important. Do not marry a person because he or she is a Christian, because there are Christians sitting in the Church who are culturally bound to their culture. When a person is culturally bound to his culture than his faith in Christ, then there is something seriously wrong with the very faith he professes.

The danger here is that some of them do not know Satan has placed a **seal of ownership on their culture.** Without breaking Satan's seal of ownership, you will be building your marriage on frozen ice, but what you do not know is the condition of the frozen ice. It may appear solid on the surface but beneath is a thin layer of ice, and all it needs is heat.

The only person in this world who can't be trusted is the devil. Therefore, whenever you pass by him be watchful and make sure he is not following you home. Satan is the architect behind some of the human cultures, traditions and customs. The devil's mark on human cultures, customs and traditions can be found in cultures that practice human sacrifice, cultures that enslave its citizens in darkness and are responsible for the backwardness of its citizens.

Jesus Christ represents the highest authority, and what He has spoken takes precedent over any other voice, whether there are of any other religious leader or some form of god. **The appearance of God in the person of Jesus Christ is what sets Christianity apart from all other religions.** Therefore, a Christian cannot go into a marriage with anyone who does not accept that Jesus Christ is the Son of God.

This reminds me of a Pastor friend who was charmed by the outward beauty of a young woman. Grandmother once said, "Outward beauty comes with is own problems." Marrying a beautiful woman is very good but what you may not know is that inwardly there is a poisonous toxic that can destroy your faith through marriage. This is what we do not know. The woman the pastor married illustrates the attitude of some Christians who think in matters pertaining to marriage, love and beauty overrides what the Scriptures forbids. This story begins in Nigeria and ends in London. During the 2003 civil war, so many Sierra-Leones escaped into the neighbouring countries. Among them was a young mother who defied all the odds and escaped by crossing two countries into Nigeria where she was granted a refugees status.

Whilst in Nigeria she was able to trace distant relatives who migrated to Nigeria in the mid-seventies who help her settle down. After settling down, she made several efforts to get in touch with the husband and children in Sierra-Leone to no avail. All the effort she made to get the family to join her in Nigeria came to a dead end. When relatives in Sierra-Leone could not trace the whereabouts of the husband and children, they presumed them dead.

Because of the savagery of war she decided to settle in Nigeria. With the help of relatives, she was able to start a small business. When the business started doing well, she moved out of the family house and rented a flat. Little did she know this move would bring her in contact with a man who would become her second husband.

One morning, while trying to cross the street to buy a loaf of bread, something on the road tripped her, but the quick reaction of a young man prevented her from falling. Was this scenario a case of providence or a mere coincidence? After the incident, they exchanged phone numbers. When the young man told her where he lived and asked her address, she replied, "I think we live two blocks from each other."

Within a matter of weeks they became friends; however, the relationship was strictly platonic. The only plausible explanation for this was that they both felt attracted to each other, but neither wanted to be the first to speak. When they could no longer hold back, they both expressed how they felt.

Within five months of their meeting the pastor proposed to the young mother and she gladly accepted his proposal. One year after he proposed, they were married and on their way to London where the young man is a Pastor of a Church. They were both very happy to be married and were looking forward to a happy life in London.

What the Pastor knew before the marriage was that the woman was a Muslim, but the tragedy of all this was that after he knew the woman's faith he went ahead and married her. By this, he had given the devil a fertile ground from which to unleash trouble in his marriage and put his ministerial career in jeopardy. Grandfather once said, "What gives the devil the greatest pleasure and joy is to ignite a fire in the marital homes of Christians, then sit back and watch them devour each other. Nothing pleases the devil better than to lead married Christians to the divorce court."

The pastor could not fathom how he got himself into a marriage that has turned so bitter in his throat. But what he did not know was that his problems had just begun. His problem was how to keep his father-in-law the devil, out of his matrimonial home. There were three things that stood between him and his marriage.

1. The culture of the woman.
2. Religion of the woman.
3. The woman was still legally married: this will turn out to be a thorn in his flesh.

The woman he married was a Muslim something he knew about before the marriage and thought he could convert her to Christianity. Christians who deliberately take what belongs to the devil and thinks they can keep it without a fight will soon find out they have started a battle they can neither win nor finish. A Christian who marries an unbeliever is spiritually blind, and there is none as blind as those who do not want to see.

How could a Pastor who is faithful to Christ deliberately marry a woman from a different faith and then expect the wife to walk away from her faith and follow a faith that she knows nothing about? A Christian who invites the devil for dinner will finish the meal with bone in his or her throat. Next time you invite the devil home for dinner, keep your eyes open before he slips a bone into your food. He who dines with the devil will not walk way from the diner table a healthy person.

The Pastor's marriage to the woman was nothing but fish bone wedged in his throat; he would live with it for the rest of his life. He would have to draw inspiration from the LORD'S words to the Apostle Paul, "My grace is sufficient for you." Sometimes when our prayers remain unanswered it is only by retracing our steps can we find the cause of the problem. Sometimes an unanswered prayer could be a test from God. An unanswered prayer does not mean we should walk away from the promises of God.

The woman became a liability in the ministry. Instead of supporting the husband's ministry she became a stumbling block. As a result, the growing Church became stagnant. The stagnation of the church continued until it started spiralling downward. Within months, the congregation started dwindling which forced the Pastor to take a paid job in order to put food on the family table and pay the bills. This is how things went from bad to worse. The Pastor had no one to blame but himself. Christians who marry from different faiths will wake up after the honeymoon to find out they have built their marriage on thin ice.

Three years into the marriage, the woman's husband (presumed to be dead) appeared from nowhere into the limelight of the Pastor's marriage and demanding to have his wife back. The drama had just begun. Unknown to the Pastor the wife had been communicating with the husband in Sierra-Leone while he was on night-duty. Without the knowledge of the Pastor the woman paid for the airfare of her elder son in Sierra-Leone to come to London.

The Pastor's stepson also became a thorn in the marriage. His activities in the house were like a fish bone wedged between the pastor's teeth. It was only the timely intervention of Christian friends who interceded in prayer for him that saved his ministry. Christian who ignores the highway-code, of the Christian marriage will surely find they are walking on thin ice. God still warns His children even though they deliberately walk into territories that are out of bounds to them.

A pastor's wife plays a very important role in the ministry and in the life of her husband. When the pastor's wife fails in this role, then it means something is wrong in the life of the pastor's wife. The role of a pastor's wife includes the following;

1. **In the Home:** the pastor's home is expected to be the role model in the home. The community in which they live know where they live and are watching them. If the community in which they live has never seen a Christian home, then their home should be the best example to the community.

2. **In the Church:** The pastor's wife must not become too involved in church positions. Her first responsibility is the parsonage, for no one

else can assume this role. She will not be able to fulfil this responsibility if she takes on too many tasks in the church. If the pastor's wife assumes too many tasks, they will limit the time that she can devote to her home. The pastor's wife should seek to be supportive of the various activities in the church. One of the duties of a Pastor's wife is to be a role model for the women in the Church. The pastor's wife must be the one who counsels women and teaches them how to be good Christian wives and homemakers. The pastor's wife must give personal support to her husband. The pastor's wife must be a faithful critic and tell her husband things that no one else can tell him. When the pastor's ministerial direction is shifting from the main reason God called him into the ministry, then it is the pastor's wife's responsibility to steer him away from material desire to the main purpose of his calling. The pastor's spiritual welfare should be something that should be of great concern to every pastor's wife.

This is a saying worth memorising: "The demon in money is greed. Nothing can destroy human beings like the passion to posses it. Money manifests itself as power. Wealth attracts people like fresh meat attracts flies. Behind money are very real spiritual forces that energize it and give it a life of its own. Hence, money is an active agent; it is a law onto itself; and it is capable of inspiring devotion. It is the ability of money to inspire that brings its dark side to the forefront."

Marriage is a good thing and you will only enjoy it if only you are married to the person God has chosen for you. On the other hand, marriage can be a bad thing when you find yourself married to the wrong person.

Marrying the wrong person spells disaster for any Christian who takes a bride outside the community of believers. The majority of Christians do not really know who they are marrying until after the honey moon is over.

The word of God is like a high way traffic signs that warns drivers of the dangers ahead of them. However, drivers who ignore these warning signs do so at their own peril. Similarly, Christians who think they can play a game of chess with the devil will soon find that the devil is smarter than they are when he gives them no chance to move.

It would have been good if God had giant sirens to warn us of an imminent attack by the devil. But He does not operate that way. Instead, we must read the Scripture daily, meditate on its truth, maintain a prayerful attitude throughout the day, and be filled with the Holy Spirit. Only then will we be sensitive to an imminent danger and be armed by the Holy Spirit so that we can resist it.

The Christian New Testament contains the explicit phrase, "Simply let your 'Yes' be 'Yes,' and your 'No' 'No';" anything beyond this is of the devil (Matthew 5:37). The call to the Christian faith is not a call to life without problems. Nevertheless, when we get distracted and find ourselves at no entry road and the devil beckons us to come and take a bride or bridegroom we must have the courage to say no.

A Christian cannot marry an unbeliever, but an unbeliever who is married to a Christian can become a Christian. In the ethics of Christian marriage, the question of **cross-religious marriage still stands as a taboo as far as the Scripture is concerned,** because the authority of the Scriptures takes precedence over personal interest.

A Christian who defies the authority of the Scriptures and marries an unbeliever is like a man who walks into blazing Tower block after watching firemen running out of the building because putting the fire out has become dangerous and hopeless. To know the Scriptures and the teaching of its moral code, then blame moral weakness for disobedience, is inexcusable.

When it comes to marriage, the Christian is set apart to be joined with a vessel that has also been set apart by the LORD, so that they become one in marriage for His glory. The prophet Amos drummed the message louder when he wrote, "Do two walk together unless they have agreed to do so?" (Amos 3:3).

God is looking for Christians marriages He can rely on. The question we should be asking is, can God rely on our marriage? The Psalmist once asked this question: "Who may ascend the hill of the LORD? Who may stand in the holy place?" The he gives the answer as, "He who has clean hands and a pure heart," God only relies on marriages that glorifies His name. When we disobey the Scriptures and marry outside the kingdom community of believers we soil the beauty of the Christian marriage.

There are so many problems in Christian marriage that those contemplating marriage should think very carefully before making the final decision. So many Christians have made mistakes by marrying unbelievers. The truth is that the Christian who marries outside the kingdom community of believers will have the devil as his father in-law. You cannot marry an unbeliever and not accept the devil as your father in-law. Your spouse will compel you to love and respect him.

Marrying an unbeliever is not an option a Christian should even consider. Not when we know the position of the Scriptures. An unbelieving spouse comes into the marriage with so much baggage including the devil as your father in-law. The storms the devil will unleash in the marriage will be beyond you. You cannot take what belongs to the devil and pretend he will have no access to your home. The tragedy of marrying an unbeliever is having the devil as your father in-law. But be warned; when things start to go wrong; do not cry out to God asking Him, "LORD! Why me, did you not see it coming, LORD? LORD, why did you not prevent it but allow me to go through all this?"

Can a Christian be married to an unbeliever? The answer is definitely no, because the Scripture is very clear on this issue. The question of Christians marrying outside the kingdom community of believers stems from the shallowness of their knowledge of the Scriptures. About sixty percent of people who claim to be Christian hardly read the Scriptures, and those who read, do not really understand basic Biblical interpretation.

One of the reasons why Christians cannot marry unbelievers can be traced to the ethics of Christian marriage. Children are God's precious jewels and Christian couples must help them shine for Christ. Christian children must raised by godly parents and be taught the Word of God right from infancy up to such time that they can be on their own.

The questions that will arise out of a cross-religious marriage are how can a Christian who is married to an unbeliever raise the children in the Christian faith and guide them to shine for Christ? On what foundation are they going to build their faith? We must not marry for our own selfish interest, knowing very well that children will come out of the marriage. Let's look at the following reasons why it will not be in our interest.

1. **Christ is the centre of praise and worship.** Therefore, it is imperative that the believer and his wife or husband worship the same God. The worshipping of God is only through Jesus Christ. If you want God to lead you and your wife or husband, then be willing to follow Christ with your spouse.
2. **Unity in Prayer:** how can a faithful believer in Jesus Christ pray with his or her spouse who is not a believer? To pray with your spouse, both of you must have the one faith, one spirit and one LORD who is Jesus Christ. Without the unity of fellowship in the family, it will be difficult to pray together in the home.
3. **Fellowship is unique In the Christian marriage:** This is the reason why a Christian should marry a Christian to ensure that fellowship with the Holy Spirit continues without interruption. How can a Christian live with his or her spouse for the rest of their life without being able to have fellowship with Christ? Without fellowship, the Christian marriage is dead because the Christian marriage thrives on fellowship with God.

For the faithful believer, Jesus Christ is the door through which we can approach God and worship Him in the spirit and in truth. How then can a Christian disobey the word of God and marry from another faith and claim he or she knows what it means to worship God? For the Christian it is through knowing Christ that we can know the full meaning of worship in our marriage. Be warned: short-term pleasures will bring long-term unhappiness and looses.

Marrying outside the Christian faith is like embarking on a suicide mission. This is a warning for

Christians who find nothing wrong in marrying outside the kingdom community of believers. People like this better think twice before they cross religious boundaries to marry outside the kingdom community of believers. Christians who value marriage and see marriage as life time commitment should marry from the kingdom community of believers to ensure fellowship with God remains unbroken.

Every religious faith is controlled by a spirit, and this is what we have to be aware of. The Christian faith is the only religion which is controlled by the Power of the Holy Spirit (Spirit of God). Other religious faith is controlled by a different spirit. Therefore, when a Christian is married to a man or woman from a different religious faith, he or she will have the spirit that controls that faith to contend with.

There are two kinds of spirits that control this world. The Spirit of God and the spirit of Satan, each of these spirits seeks to use the human body as its dwelling place, and then control the body. Their control of the human body is through religion. Hence the reason why we have so many religious faiths in this world, and even within each religious faith there are so many denominations. Religious denominations are the breeding grounds for spirits.

The battle for the control of the human body begins with religious worship. The difference between these two spirits is that the spirit of Satan seeks worship, while the Holy Spirit directs worship to God. This is the reason why God forbid Jews from cross-religious marriage, because cross-religious leads to the worship of foreign gods or familiar spirits. The greatest form of idolatry is when worship of an evil spirit is substituted for the worship of God. If Satan fails to substitute a material god for the true God, he will substitute a god of spirit.

If a Christian marries from a different religion, whatever spirit controls the religion of his or her spouse will control the marriage. The most dangerous situation in a marriage is to have two spirits controlling the marriage. Grandfather once told me that, "The Spirit of God cannot dwell in the heart of a redeemed man with the devil except with Christ."

Grandfather once said, "Show me the way you live and I will tell you the kind of God you are worshipping." It is true that when a Christian marries a man or woman from a different religious faith, the spirit that controls that religion will change his or her character. God desires for Christian marriage is to make the couple look like Jesus.

Grandfather once told me that, "Two of the highest joys that come from worship are fellowship with God and personal transformation." How then, can a Christian whose spouse is from a different religion be able to experience the joy of fellowship with God through Jesus Christ? The Holy Spirit gives inexpressible joy when a married Christian couple are joined in the unity of fellowship and worship.

The marriage between Ali, a devout Muslim, and Naomi, a Christian, is a typical example of how some Christian marriages turn into a suicide mission. Christians who cross religious barriers because of love will be confronted with either death or divorce. A Christian woman who crosses the religious divide to marry must be aware that some religions have no respect for women and as such treat women as a slave.

The story we are about to read illustrates the consequences of marrying outside the kingdom community of believer. This is a story of a young beautiful Christian girl who married her fiancé against the will of her devout Christian parents. The parents opposed the marriage on the grounds that her fiancé was from a different faith. Yet she stubbornly refused to see reason.

The marriage of Naomi and Ali was a tragic mistake which took her to an early grave. Why this Christian could be blinded by love and marry a beast from a different religious faith will remain a mystery. Her reason for marrying this beast will remain buried with her in the grave. She is not here to defend herself, therefore, it is best to remain silent and not disturb her burial ground.

After giving birth to three beautiful daughters and a son, the husband started bringing mistresses to the matrimonial home whenever she visited her parents. When Naomi confronted the husband about the mistresses, she got the beating of her life. It was only the timely intervention of her children that saved her.

He told Naomi that as a Muslim he was entitled to marry up to four women and there was nothing she could do about it. Here, the man himself has erred because there is a clause inserted in the edict that allows followers of Islam to marry more than one wife if only they can take care of them. Beside, the edict does not ask them to have mistresses. Nothing is more revealing of this man's true character than the lust of the flesh. The only thing that would make a man marry more than one wife is the lust of the flesh. Marrying more than one wife is like a school of adversity that distinguishes failure from success.

Temptation is like fire; it consumes some things and purifies others. Temptation is like a raging fire that destroys anything in its path. For a married man to be tempted to take more than one wife only shows two things, the love and desire for his wife has diminished or his uncontrolled lust for women is tempting him to take many wives.

When it finally dawned on her she was up against a religion whose views of marriage were different than her own she resign herself to it as her fate. This is what Christians who think it is possible to mix water with oil will be confronted with. Water is water, so is oil, when you mix both of them in bottle and shake the contents it only takes a few seconds for the water to be separated from the oil. Similarly, you cannot mix Christianity with another religion through marriage and expect something unique. A religion that allows its followers to take more than one wife is a religion that desecrates the spirit of marriage. A religion that advocates polygamous marriage is a religion that channels lust through marriage.

When Naomi was eight months pregnant with her fifth child, her husband beat her and pushed her so hard that she fell flat on her stomach. As a result, she collapsed and was rushed to hospital. Three weeks after she was discharged from the hospital, the husband resumed the beating. This time doctors had to induce labour. As the result of these two incidents, the baby was born brain damaged. After the birth of the baby, she developed high blood-pressure and diabetes. Three years after the birth of the baby, Naomi died, killed by the beast she married. The most dreadful thing about marriage is to be killed by no other person than the person you married. We marry to love and be loved, we marry to cherish and be cherished and we marry to desired and be desired. These are the words of my grandmother when I married. The passion of lusting after what does not belong to us is what will make a husband or wife kill their spouse in order to have what he or she been secretly desiring.

A week after her funeral, this man sat on the matrimonial bed, crying, "What a fool I have been. I have killed my wife, I have killed my wife." Has this man any conscience? I think the answer is no. Conscience may trouble a person because of real guilt or because of irrational guilt. When the conscience is troubled by real guilt, it affects a person's relationship with God.

Guilt is a feeling resulting from going against truth. When a person's religion does not teach how God has revealed His truth in His Word, then his religion lacks substance. For the Christian, we know that God has revealed truth to us in the Word of God (John 17:17). Truth is one, whole and complete, is only revealed to man by God.

Naomi went into this forbidden marriage with Christian values, which meant submitting to her husband. On the other hand, the husband's religion regards women submitting to their husband as a matter of status, which is one person being above another or hierarchy (a master-slave relationship). In Naomi's faith that is not the case, but rather deals with role and function.

Naomi married her husband without checking her husband's cultural background. It was only after the wedding that she realised she had married a man from a culture and a religion that accepts wife beating as part of the marriage. Some male dominated cultures wrongly view women as nothing more than property or sexual objects. Women have historically been relegated to the role of cooking, cleaning, and child bearing by some cultures.

In another example, we will take the story of a Muslim young woman who married a Christian in a colourful wedding. The marriage was doom to fail before it even started because it was opposed by the parents of the young man. The young man's parents opposed the marriage for two reasons 1, the religion of their son's fiancée and 2, the cultural background of the woman. Is this a good reason for parents to oppose their son or daughter's marriage?

The Christian young man ignored his parent's opposition of marrying his Turkish girlfriend. This young man could not resist the beauty of the young Muslim woman; as a result he disobeyed his parents' advice. Let me sound a warning from my grandfather, "Men and women who marry without their parents' blessing are likely to run into problems later in the marriage."

During their wedding reception the young man was all over his wife, kissing and cuddling her. This made the newly wedded wife ask him a question that would one day become the test of his love for her. The question his beautiful Muslim wife asked was, "Will this love, affection and cuddling continue throughout our marriage?"

The Christian husband said, "Yes," He kept the promise he made to his wife on the day of their wedding. Nevertheless, seven years after the after marriage, the spark that lit the flame to join the two hearts together started to dim. Then gradually the bright light in the marriage died out. The sensible thing the Christian husband could have done was pray to God to rekindle the bright flame that shone early in the marriage.

On their seventh wedding anniversary, they spent the weekend with the husband's family. As the family sat down enjoying the party, the D J played the husband's favourite song, which happened to be the very song that the husband chose to be played on their wedding reception. At this, the wife got up, kissed her husband on the lips and asked for a dance. What happen next was unexpected and unprepared for. The shock was enough to tell her the end was near.

The husband pushed her away, and as if that was not enough he told her, "You are being stupid." The shellshock wife moved away quietly and sat among in-laws who had never welcomed her into the family. When they arrived home the wife was expecting an apology from her husband, but it never came. The worst behaviour in marriage is when a spouse offends his wife or husband and then pretends as if nothing has happened. When she asked the husband, "Why did you spurn me in the mist of so many people?" His reply was bluntly, "It is not in my nature to do what you asked for or to be seen kissing my wife in the presence of my family."

The words of this Christian husband can be attributed to nothing but deception. For the years that he had been married to his wife, he lived a life of deception by pretending to be what he was not. We cannot suppress what we are not forever, because it will eventually show up someday, because certain inconsistencies in our life will give us up. And that's what happened to this young man.

Is he a Christian as he claims? If he is, then why did he cross religious boundaries to marry a woman from a different religion? If after seven years of marriage his faith in Christ could not lead his beautiful wife to the Saving grace of our LORD Jesus Christ, then we should be doubtful of the very faith he professes in Christ. As a Christian he should be fully conversant with what the Scriptures teach about how a husband should behave toward his wife. The behaviour of some Christians in marriage is worst than that of unbelievers and it reveals what they are really made of.

The behaviour of this man is like a man who slips a bullet into an empty barrel of a gun his enemies have been pointing at his marriage. His family had been pointing an empty gun at his marriage and all they needed was the bullet in his hand. This man claimed to be a Christian yet forgot that it was the responsibility of the Christian husband to love and cherish his wife.

The behaviour of this man reminds me of when Alexander the Great asked the Greek philosopher Diogenes what he could do for him, Diogenes replied, "Stand out of my sunlight." Let us see in this reply an exhortation for us to put aside anything that would dim the light in our marriage and instead fan the flame that will relight the marriage vows.

The purpose of the marriage vow is to remind married a couple of their commitment to each order "Till death do us part." Learning more about what is involved in marriage and its requirements and abiding by its principles will help married couples love and cherish each order and remain committed to upholding the vows. The basic requirement of the marriage vow is that married spouse will embrace faithfulness, love, affection and walk in the holiness of the marriage without breaking the vow. Vows that are made by a married couple are meant to be binding.

Christian husbands must live by their marriage vows in a manner that pleases God who instituted marriage. It is the first necessary approach to a happy marital relationship. With the Christian marriage, spiritual and physical purification of both spouses are not separable, however we may safely say that the whole tenor of Scripture indicates God's concern with spiritual purification and physical purification of marriage.

Nevertheless, it is only through the cleansing power of the blood of Jesus Christ and His Word that the Christian marriage going through difficulties can be cured from sin and freed from bondage. For the marriage, holiness is the basic requirement of God's approval and divine protection for the Christian marriage.

Lack of unity within cross-cultural marriage today is frequently the causes of divorce. Beside, the very nature of marriage vows should cause fear and trembling in the heart of committed Christians who have promised to uphold the marriage vows. The desire to please God in our marriage should instil holy reverence for God in the heart of those who know Him and are striving to uphold the marriage institution God ordained.

In marriage we are looking for peace, comfort, and security. This is what every Christian woman expects in marriage. And it is the responsibility of the Christian husband to ensure that his wife enjoys the comfort of the Christian home. However, the Christian woman is unlikely to find this in other religions.

Reading through a devotional book, I came across the following headings, "**TEMPTING OUTSIDE; TOXIC INSIDE.**" Since we do not know what is inside a person, we must depend on God alone who knows the toxicity of a person's life. Physical appearance can be very deceptive, and fools are carried away by it. In a world where people cannot be trusted to speak the truth, the Holy Spirit is the only person we can trust to reveal what has been concealed by the person you want to commit yourself to.

The human life is toxic; therefore what comes out of us is also toxic. The toxicity can only cleansed by the blood of Jesus Christ. How then can a Christian marry a person from another faith, knowing that that person has not been cleansed by the blood of Jesus? It takes the purifying blood of Jesus to make a Christian husband or wife who he or she is.

However, Christians who stubbornly walk into doomed marriages by crossing religious barriers to marry a man or woman whose toxic life has not been cleansed by Jesus will find himself or herself in a marriage marred by the toxic life his or her spouse. A religion can look very beautiful and attractive from outside, but what is inside can be full of poison.

A religion can be like a tree of beliefs whose flowers are quite pretty to look at, but when you squeeze them, they give off an unpleasant odour. Christians who marry from other religions should be aware that, the by-products of some religions are very toxic. If we cannot find what we are looking for in the Church, and decide to look outside the kingdom community of believers, then we are bound to run into problems.

What attracts a person into marriage may turn to joy or sorrow, honour or disgrace, life or death. God has setup spiritual boundaries for His children, but those who foolishly cross the boundary have put themselves outside God's protective zone. A tragic mistake that has taken some Christians to their early grave; we must all try to avoid cross-religious marriage.

Cross-religious marriage raises fundamental questions about the reasons why some Christians think there is nothing wrong with such marriage. Two lines of thought worth considering in these issues are;

1. Commitments to the Christ.
2. Obedience to the Word of God.

We live in a world of "you scratch by back and I'll scratch your back." This is how some Christians live their lives. For many, this principle of give –and –take extends to their faith in God. Ask them why they believe in God and they will reply that it is because of all the wonderful things God has done for them. In effect, their walk with God operates on the basis of reciprocity: He gives to them, and in exchange they follow Him. Do you follow God because of the "reward" you believe He has given you? Suppose you have been praying for a wife or husband and He is silent over your request. What will you do? Walk away and find any woman from any religious faith? Cross-religious marriage raises fundamental questions about fellowship, faith, broken marriages, suffering and the extent to which human beings can understand God's way.

The only way Christians can avoid bad marriages is by embracing God's wisdom and godly advise to guide them. It is only by waiting on God that we can avoid foolish choices in marriage. It will interest you to know that there are no Scriptural verses to support cross religious marriage. God's stance on such a marriage is absolute.

Even within the Christian community, we have to be very careful when it comes to cross-cultural marriage. For example, you come from Angola and you meet a Christian from Nigeria in your local church and you both fall in love and decide to marry without checking each other's cultural background.

Culture is something we cannot ignore in marriage just because we are Christians. Therefore, the consent of both cultures must be sought and agreed before a Christian couple should be married. Extensive research shows that most marital problems are spiritual rather than physical, and in this, Christians involved in cross-cultural marriages suffer the worst.

Courting Christians whose partner comes from a different culture need to spent time in knowing each other's culture, customs and tradition. Otherwise if you get married without getting the approval of both families, you may face spiritual problems in the marriage. Where culture stands in the way of a courting couple, they have to spend time in prayer to know the will of God.

Today there are many cross-cultural Christian marriages facing problems. I have counselled many people involved in cross-cultural marriage and results shows that many of them are facing problems. Some have fasted and prayed without surmounting the problems. The problem here is that without knowing the root cause of the problem you are encountering in your marriage you may not be able to deal with the problem.

The person you want to marry may have been dedicated to a god or shrine before he or she became a Christian. And this is where the problem starts and is also the place to start from. However, some Christians assume once they have surrendered their lives to Christ, then they no longer have a problem with the devil. Christians like these needs to be reminded that our problem with devil starts from the day we gave our life to Christ.

If you come from a family that is involved in any of the following, idol-worshiping, occult, Freemasons, or any of the brotherhood lodges, then after your conversion, you will need deliverance. Christians who come from such families have to make their pastor aware of this.

The beginning of our problems start from the day we switch from the kingdom of darkness to the kingdom of light. From that day onwards we become the subject of attention of the devil. He will not relent until he succeeds in bringing us back to his domain. Is it possible for a Christian to be influenced by the devil? Oh yes!

It is important that when a person becomes a Christian he or she must break away from every family idol-worshiping. The devil does not easily give up on what once belongs to him. Even when you become a Christian, the devil comes after you and your family.

Dedication to the devil involves a blood sacrifice which seals a bond between you and the shrine you were dedicated to. It does not matter whether it was done when you were an infant or an adult, with or without your consent. As long your father, mother or any member of the family stood on your behalf and performed the sacrifice; it will still have effect on your spiritual life or influence your life as a Christian.

Some family would not need your consent before carrying out the sacrifice on your behalf, however some families will just go ahead and perform the rituals and then tell you that they have performed sacrifice to the family shrine on your. Immediately they tell you this you have to publicly denounce the sacrifice, by telling them who you are in Christ, and that you have nothing to do with the dedication.

Denunciations are not enough. You must make sure you live a live worthy of your calling and not create an opportunity in your life for custodians of the shrine to create problems in your marital home. Sin is the only open door that can allow the devil to enter a Christian's life. Do not under estimate the spiritual power of a family shrine.

A pastor friend once told me the following story of how a person can be held captive by sin. He said, a farmer went to work on his farm one morning and saw sin running toward him as if something was after his life. The farmer asked sin, "Who is after you that has made you run for your life? Then sin said, "It is the devil. He wants to make me his servant, but I want nothing to do with him. Please could you give me a place to hide where the devil will not see me?" At this, the farmer asked sin, "Where are you going to hide that the devil will not find you? The sin said, "You stomach."

Then the farmer asked, "How?" Then sin said, "Open your mouth so that I can pass through your mouth into your stomach." Then the farmer asked sin, "What happens after the devil goes away?" Then sin said, "As soon as the devil goes away I will come out." The farmer opened his mouth and sin entered his stomach. As soon as sin was safe in the farmer's stomach, the farmer saw the devil coming toward him. Then the farmer asked Satan, "What are looking for on my farm?" Then, the devil said, "I am looking for sin to make him my agent, have you seen him?" Then the farmer said, "I saw sin running toward that way, pursue him if you are lucky you may overtake him and make him your agent."

As soon as the devil was gone and the farmer saw that it was safe for sin to come to come out, he told sin, "It is now safe for you to come out because the devil is gone" Then sin replied, "How can I come out when it is safe and comfortable here." Then the farmer reminded sin of his promise to come out as soon as the devil was out of sight. At this, sin said, "Yes I did promise to come out, but that was then, because I did not know how safe and comfortable your stomach would be." The farmer kept insisting for sin to come out, sin said to the farmer, "Can I ask you a question?" The farmer said, "Yes." Then sin said, "Would you come out of a fortress where you know you are comfortable and safe from your enemies?" This is how sin works its way into our lives.

If the man or woman you want to marry has been dedicated to a shrine from infancy without knowing it, then this can still pose a problem. This is the reason why you have to know more about the family background of the person you want to marry. For as long as he or she has not been delivered from the spirit that controls the shrine, he or she belongs to the devil and there is nothing you can do to stop Satan from coming to your home.

For example, your parents have been married for years without children, and as a result they consulted the spirit world for help and you were born. Remember the devil gives nothing for nothing. Satan will surely demand a pound of flesh, and it is your soul. When a person in this state becomes born-again Christian, he or she will have a spiritual battle on their hands.

A Christian born as a result of the parents seeking the help of a river goddess, spiritualist or through the consultation of the spirit world would surely have marital problems. Some of the spirits from whom your parents consulted for help will not easily give up on you. These spirits are very jealous and would not want any competition.

These spirits will stop at nothing until they succeeds in destroying your marriage. When they succeed in coming into your home, they cause havoc in the marriage by using weapon at their disposal, such as an unforgiving spirit, quick temperament spirit, and spirit of anger where you find yourself unable to control your anger. When these things are happening in your marriage then know that you are being influenced by familiar spirits. Spirit of provocation where you become quarrelsome person, a Christian husband or wife who is always quarrelling is not a good ambassador of Christ.

Some of these spirits target your finances so that anything you do becomes a failure. They cause problem in your business or work. Their aim is to cause poverty in your home. In a nutshell these spirits have a wide range of weapons at their disposal to use against your marriage. If you are very observant you will notice the early warning signs in your dreams.

A Christian husband or wife who was born as a direct result of the intervention of these spirits will have to set their ears to hear God's voice, hand to render service to God, and feet to maintain a daily walk of holiness. In times of spiritual conflict, we need a husband who is in touch with God. Holiness safeguards our personal relation with God. God has always wanted His people to live in a happy marriage without their marriage being influence by evil spirits.

I know an English family that went to East Africa on holidays and came back with a curved wooden idol representing a fertility god. From the day they placed the carved image in their living room, the woman has had one miscarriage to another. Medically, this baffled their family doctor who referred them to a gynaecologist. Test carried out on her showed there was nothing medically wrong with her.

Then one day, a young Christian woman who comes from the very town in East Africa where they bought the wooden carving came to baby-sit for them. When she saw the fertility carving she knew it was the cause of the frequent miscarriages. She told her friend who recommended her to tell the couple what she thought was the causes of the miscarriages.

The family attribute the baby-sitters advice as to mere superstition. It was only when the husband decided to temporarily remove the carving from the house that they saw the truth in what they baby-sitter had been saying. When the miscarriages stopped they burned the carving. And that was the end of the problem in the family.

This young woman knew from personal experience wood carvers from her native town invoke spirit into the carving to attract people to buy them. The spirit they invoke into the curving are not ordinary spirit, they are demonic spirit that can bring curses or blessings to the person who buys the wooden carving. Blessing in this context has nothing to do with divine blessing. Satan's material blessing does not come without a condition. Your soul and body is what he will need in exchange.

In another example, a South American Christian friend suddenly started experiencing unexpected problems in his marriage. The problem first started with his finances. When the devil attacks your source of income, he knows it is where you are vulnerable and the most likely place to bring you down. The Scriptures describes money as the source of all of evil. (1st Timothy 6:10).From here, the problem spread, further affecting his children, who suddenly became very disobedient.

His business, that had been doing very well, nose-dived, as a result his accountants advised him to wind down the business because it was no longer profitable to run. The folding up of the business triggered a wave of uncontrolled problems in the home that nearly caused the break-up of the marriage. He and his wife started praying and fasting for answers.

When the problems got beyond them they spoke to their pastor who got the church prayer warrior team involved. The Church prayer warriors were assigned to intercede for the family. After prolonged months of praying, the answer finally came in a form of vision, while they were praying in the home of the Christian Brother.

The Lord opened the spiritual eye of one of the sisters in the prayer warrior team to a beautiful crystal glass in the living room which was a wedding gift. The crystal glass came from his ancestral family idol temple and had been passed from one generation to the other. The crystal glass became a source of blessing to its custodian as long as the person performs certain rituals.

However, for some unknown reason the crystal glass given to him as a wedding present was shrouded in mystery. He was not told the mystery that surrounded the crystal glass. Family members told him that the beautiful crystal glass was responsible for his booming business that brought him wealth. He rejected this claim because he could not reconcile how such a glass could be responsible for his wealth. In his own words he said, "I have no knowledge the crystal glass belongs to the devil and as such required rituals sacrifices."

On the advice of the leader of the prayer warrior team, the crystal glass was returned to head of the family because it was a family property that has passed from one generation to another. Once the crystal glass was removed from the house the link that connected him to the crystal glass was broken. From then onwards the problems in the family stopped.

What we must know is that, a Christian cannot keep what belongs to the devil and expect him not to have unrestricted access to his home. Once you take what belongs to the devil, whether knowingly or unknowingly, you cannot stop him from being a guest in your home. You will be wasting your time fasting and praying until you return what belongs to him.

Objects with satanic connection attract spirits from the spirit world, while those dedicated to family shine are to protect the family. Therefore, whoever has that object in his or her possession become the custodian of the object and must protect it with his or her soul. Idols are not gods; precisely the opposite. They are the habitations of demonic powers. Some people have objects dedicate to gods or shrines in their possession without knowing and this can cause problems in the marriage.

Some Christians involved in cross-cultural marriage may face marital problems because of object dedicated to gods in their possession. To avoid a troubled marriage, Christians who marry outside their culture should endeavour to research the cultural background of their spouse. Object dedicated to a family shrine can turn out to be the source of the problem in their marriage.

Those who know they are in possession of objects or object dedicated to shrine before becoming Christian should dispose of them once they become Christians. From the day you become a Christian you invoke the fury of the evil spirit who owns the objects in your possession because you have something that belongs to them. The object dedicated to the shrine is what belongs to them.

You may be given something like a ring, earrings or necklace given to you by a member of your family without knowing where the items came from. The item you cherish so much may have been dedicated to a shrine you don't know anything about. Items like gold jewellery that have been in family possession and have passed from one generation to the next are likely to have been dedicated to shrines. This does not imply all Jewellery that has been passed from one generation to the other has been dedicated to idols.

Items like these cannot be sold because certain pronouncements might have been invoked on them. If you have such items in your possession given to you by a member of your family, it will be worth finding out its history. Remember the devil knows things in your home that belongs to him, and as long as those things are in your possession he has unrestricted assess to your home.

The Real Nature of Idolatry: the worship of idols does not just refer to the act of bowing to a physical object. The Bible also speaks of a spiritual form: the idolatry of the heart. It describes greed as idolatry (Colossians 3:5). The greedy person acquires things to satisfy himself. This indicates that spiritual idolatry is a form of self-worship. This self-worship is also the basis for the worship of a physical idol.

Idol worshipers want to obtain some favour from "gods." These favours may be such things as protection, prosperity and good marriage. Their worship is self-centred rather than God centred. Therefore, we can say that the real nature of all idolatry is spiritual rather than physical. Christians, who have the image of God renewed in them, must therefore shun all forms of idolatry.

Anything in your possession that links you to a shrine is the binding cord that needs to be broken before you can be free from demonic spirits. Your only way to victory is the immediate return of everything in your possession that links to the shrine. It could be something you might have swallowed during the time of your ignorance. God can deliver you from it. All you have to do is to tell God what you have done, although He knows you have swallowed something that belongs to the devil. Acknowledging what we have done in the past, for example, taking a vow before a shrine, dedicating your life to the shrine or taking an oath of allegiance before a shrine.

You may have been dedicated to a shrine or river goddess because of the circumstances in which you were born. Let's take an instance where your parents were childless, and in their desperation to have a child, they consulted the shrine or river god for help. Then the gods "answer their prayers." So you were born as the result of this consultation.

Just as "Only God knows those who are His" similarly, Satan also knows those who have something in them that belongs to him and he will not relent until he has total control over whatever he knows belongs to him. Denouncing the devil is the first step to freeing yourself from his clutches and having a happy marriage without demonic influence.

If you think because you are a Christian, you come under the direct protection of God so those spirits cannot cause trouble in your marriage, then you don't know the kind of spirit you are dealing with or you are blind to the Word of God. Being a Christian does not make you immune to demonic attacks. Great men of God like Paul all experienced some form of satanic attacks.

To find an answer to the problem in your marriage, first you need to find out if the problem you are facing is spiritual or physical. How do you know if the problem is physical or spiritual? Your dreams will hold some answers, because dreams are one of the media through which God speaks to His children. In dreams God reveals the devil's evil plans against your marriage.

Dreams are messages being communicated to us. How we react to the dreams will either help to avert danger or fulfil the dream. Our quest to seek the meaning of the dream will play a crucial role in resolving the message being communicated. It is quite natural to share dreams with others, especially with members of our family or friends. However, we must be very careful of the kind of people we discuss our dreams with because dreams foretell future events. Therefore, if the dream contains information that can provoke others to jealousy and envy, we must hold back and say nothing.

Dreams deals with spiritual revelations, because in dreams God is communicating a message from the spiritual realms. Because we are human, we are limited in knowledge of what goes on in the spiritual realms. What goes on in the spiritual realm is not something humans can easily comprehend or retrieve, because it is a knowledge hidden from us but available to spirits.

Some of this knowledge is available to Satan and his demons and they can use it to wage spiritual conflict against us. The fact that this knowledge is available to them does not mean they can prevent your destiny from happening. They can only delay it. However, in some instances the delay can be to your advantage. *The word delay is the devil's trump card.* He and his demons use it to frustrate us into walking away before the blessing comes.

The good news is that God has placed a limitation on the inhabitants of the spiritual realms on how far they can access this knowledge and use it against us. Even if they are able to access it through God's permissive rule, God is the one who decides the extent that knowledge can be used. Unless God permits Satan and his demons, they cannot use the knowledge they hold about us to harm as.

How do we interpret dreams? Some dreams are very easy to understand or interpret, while others come in coded messages. Dreams that are revealed in coded messages are difficult to understand or interpret. They can only be interpreted with divine help. Examples of dreams that come in coded messages can be found in Genesis Chapter 40 and 41 and in Daniel Chapters 2, 4 and the vision in Chapter 5.

Dreams do not come by chance, neither is it a natural occurrence that happens in everyone's life. In dreams, a higher being is communicating a future message. That higher being is God who alone can reveal mysteries to those He wishes to communicate that message with. From Scriptures we can confidently say God communicates with man through dream, visions and prophecy, at other times through direct revelation. An example of direct revelation can be found in the book of Daniel Chapter 5, where the finger of a human hand appeared and wrote on the plaster wall.

The Oxford Dictionary defines a dream as a series of images, events and feelings that happen in the mind while you are asleep. This is a human definition; from this, one will simply regard dreams as nothing but human feelings. Are all dreams a means of divine revelation? The answer is no, not all dreams are direct revelation from God. We need divine counsel in discerning dreams in order to separate the chaff from the grain.

Marriage was designed to bring joy, happiness and hope. However, some people become frustrated and look forward to a better happy marriage only to find darkness and gloom, broken dreams, broken marriage and dashed hope. In this life the fulfilment of a happy marriage is never certain. But one day our deepest desires and longings and the perfect fulfilment in a happy marriage will be in heaven.

The blindness in cross-cultural marriage is something we cannot see beyond. What we know is the person we want to be married to, but the person's culture, customs, and tradition are obscure to us. This blindness is what we must wake up to and ask God to open our spiritual eyes to.

In cross-cultural marriage, knowing everything about your spouse is not enough, you must also know everything about his or her culture, custom and tradition. These three areas are the trouble spot and where problems in the marriage are likely to come from. People in cross-cultural marriage should not look beyond these areas when problems start in the marriage.

Problems that start in cross-cultural marriage are linked to or connected to any of the three above. Problems in cross-cultural marriage start because of our inability to know the culture, customs and the traditions of our spouse. In the cosmopolitan society there is the possibility of people marrying outside their culture. While there is nothing wrong in marrying outside your culture, caution must be the key word.

Turning to the Scripture, we see an example of men from a particular race who married from a different culture purely because the women who came from a different culture were more beautiful than women from their culture. Their action to take other women outside their culture as wives led to "The Flood." Let's take up the story from Genesis. "When men began to increase in number on the earth and daughters were born to them, the sons of God saw that the daughters of men were beautiful, and they married any of them they chose.

Then the Lord said, "My Spirit will not content with man for ever, for he is mortal; his days will be a hundred and twenty years. The Nephilim were on the earth in those days and also afterwards when the sons of God went to the daughters of men and had children by them. They were the heroes of old, men of renown.

The Lord saw how great man's wickedness on the earth had become, and that every inclination, on of the thoughts of his heart was only evil all the time. The Lord was grieved that he had made man on the earth, and his heart was filled with pain. So the Lord said, "I will wipe mankind, whom I have created, from the face of the earth, men and animals, and creatures that move along the ground, and birds of the air for I am grieved that I have made them."

Who were these sons of God? Bible scholars differ about who the "son of God" were who married the

216

"daughters of men." Some think they were angelic beings. Others believe they were men of the godly line of Seth. Still others think were men who believe in God, whether Sethites or other descendants of Adam. Consider these three possible explanations of the "son of God."

Angels. The book of Job calls angels "sons of God," The New Testament speaks of fallen angels (Jude 6, 2 Peter 2:4). Some scholars think these fallen angels were "sons of God" who married women. Their sons were giants, the Nephilim. However, Jesus implied that angels are sexless: "At the resurrection people will neither marry nor be given in marriage; they will be like the angels in heaven" (Matthew 22:30).

While Scriptures indicate that angels are spirits, there are several examples of their visits to people when they took on human form. Even if they did have appearance of men, this does not mean that they could have sexual relations with women or that they could father a hybrid of half man and half angel.

2. Believers. The Bible calls the followers of the Lord His children or sons (Deuteronomy 32:5; Psalms 73:15; 80:17; Hosea 1:10). Some scholars think the "sons of God" were believers (whether Sethites or descendants of Adam) who married on the basis of physical attraction alone (Genesis 6:2), whether the women were godly or ungodly. This has been a cause of spiritual decline throughout history and is still today. This view seems to fit the Bible and reality better than the fallen angel theory.

3. Sethites. Some scholars see the "sons of God" as the Sethites and the "daughters of men" as the Cainite women. In this theory, intermarriage between the godly line of Seth and the evil line of Cain brought the moral ruin of the race. This third theory has two problems. First, intermarriage between Cainites and Sethites

would not affect the other descendants of Adam, who were probably the majority of the population. Second, godliness is a matter of individual choice, not of heredity. Furthermore; the Bible does not teach that all Cainites were evil or that all Sethites were godly.

One thing we know for sure is that the choice of wives by the sons of God was based on physical appeal. The women were beautiful, and that was all that they cared about. Naturally these mixed marriages ended in disaster. Since godless mothers could not teach their children the true way, the foundations of godliness began to crumble, morals decayed, and violence followed. Godless men became immoral men; immoral men became cruel men; cruel men became violent men and so violence filled the earth!

Satan has followed the same pattern throughout history. He attacks the home by promoting sensuality through preoccupation with physical beauty and sex. He breaks down the moral standards and faith in God. Then he leads people into self-centred living, violence, and crime. This pattern has led to the death of many civilizations. Even today this pattern threatens the destruction of modern civilization in many nations.

Today broken marriages and unhealthy family relationships, going one's own way in defiance of God's will for us, strife and violence in our cities and rejection of the Biblical message of Christian faith all points to the reason for which we marry. When a Christians marries on the basis of the physical appearance, he breaks the moral code of Biblical principles.

The consequences of marrying with the wrong motive embroiled other creatures that had nothing to do with man's lusting after the flesh. When it comes to marriage, the attitude of what men were before the flood and after the flood is no different from the attitude of men in this present evil generation. When it comes to marriage, history is repeating itself, because those who forget history are likely to repeat it.

The writer of this book is no way writing against cross-cultural marriage; far from it, rather he seeks emphasis the need to avoid the pitfalls that can plague spouses' involved cross-cultural marriages. The fact that you are a Christian does not mean you can brush aside issues in marriage that involve culture, customs and traditions.

A person's culture identifies him or her heritage. Therefore, being a Christian does not mean we should have nothing to do with it. It is only when certain part of our culture conflicts with our faith that we don't have to compromise. Where nothing about our faith is threatened by customs and traditions then we can go ahead and marry. On the other hand, if the unsaved members of our families want to impose certain traditions that run contrary to the Word of God, then we must resist.

For the Christian, there is nothing morally or spiritually wrong in marrying a Christian who is from a different culture, as long as your motive of marrying from another culture is right with God's purpose for you. Do not marry from another culture because women from that culture are more beautiful than women from your culture or because of that culture's rich heritage. This is what the LORD told Judah for his unfaithfulness, "Judah has broken faith. A detestable thing has been committed in Israel and in Jerusalem: Judah has desecrated the sanctuary the LORD loves, by marrying the daughters of a foreign god."

THE NATURE OF THE CHRISTIAN MARRIAGE

Newlyweds bring a variety of expectations to marriage. But what are God's expectations for the marriage relationship? He designed the institution. What did He have in mind when He established it? One window on God's perspective comes from His own "marriage" to Israel. Isaiah portals the relationship between the Lord and His people as a marriage (Isaiah (62:1-5). Notice what God as the Bridegroom does for His bride.

1. He protects and purifies her.
2. He honours and values her.
3. He identifies Himself with her, as signified by giving her new names.

Centuries later, Paul echoed Isaiah's bridal portrait of God and Israel when he described the marriage between Christ and the church (Eph. 5:21-33). Once again, the Bridegroom shows His love by protecting and purifying His bride, honouring and valuing her, and identifying Himself with her. Paul exhorted Christians to build their marriages on a similar basis.

Is this how you view marriage? Do you see it as a high and holy calling to serve your spouse in the ways described? This is the heart of a Biblical foundation of marriage. There can be no greater love and commitment expressed between husband and wife than to exhibit the character that God has shown toward Israel and that Christ has shown toward the church. Furthermore, this is an important reason for a believer to marry a believer, knowing that one partner holds himself or herself accountable to God for the other's well-being.

Have you ever listened to half of a telephone conversation, trying to figure out what the whole conversation is about? That's what we have in 1 Corinthians 7. Half, of a very important conversation on marriage between Paul and the Corinthians believers. But we can glean through many practical lessons from this passage, for marriage was undergoing profound changes then, just as it is today.

Some believers in the early church had married before they became Christians. They wondered whether they should divorce their unbelieving spouses in order to remarry Christians and live more wholeheartedly for Christ. An argument could be made for that. After all, if people's primary loyalty were now to Jesus, shouldn't that invalidate their preconversion marriage vows? (Of course, it would also provide them with a convenient excuse to escape bad marriages.

But Paul didn't recommend that. He viewed the abandonment of one's family as a very serious matter (1 Corinthians 7:10-11), arguing that the believer should stay in the marriage as long as possible (7:12-13). However, God desires peace in relationship (7:15), and that may not be possible in a family where Christian values are not shared. If the unbeliever wants to leave, he or she should be allowed to do so (7:15).

Many churches in different cultures around the world today are faced with the very similar circumstance. For example:

1. The new believer who wonders what to do, since her husband is not interested in church or religion.

2. The inner-city congregation that has members who live in common-law marriage. What should the church tell them?
3. The recent immigrant who tells his pastor that he has two families, one in each of two countries. "Should I get rid of one or both of those families?"
4. A tribal chief who wants to join the church, along with his five wives. What should he do with the wives? Should he get rid of them all? Keep one? Which one?
5. A new believer who has fathered children with a woman he lives with.
6. A woman in cohabitating relationship who has now become a believer, but has children with the man.

Paul offers no simple solutions for any of these situations, but he does share one piece of very good news: it is possible for one believer to "sanctify" a family, that is, to be an agent of God's love and grace, and perhaps eventually bring other family members into the faith. No matter how unconventional the situation might be, Scripture doesn't counsel sudden changes. God may have work left to do in the family, and He may use the believer to do it, if he or she stays.

Now let's turn our attention to the following Scriptural verses. Do not be yoked together with unbelievers. For what do righteousness and wickedness have in common? Or what fellowship can light have with darkness? What harmony is there between Christ and Belial? What does a believer have in common with an unbeliever? What agreement is there between the temple of God and idols? For we are the temple of the living God. (2 Corinthians 6:14-16).

This passage certainly refers to marriage. A Christian should not marry an unsaved person. The name **Belial** means "worthlessness." Here it is the name for the evil one. Can there be peace between Christ and Satan? Obviously not! Neither can there be fellowship between a **Believer and an unbeliever.** To attempt it is treason against the Lord.

Marriage brings a man and a woman together. Marriage is indeed a great unifier. It is a solemn, respectable institution created by God Himself, and it joins together a man and a woman in amazing oneness. Marriage brings a man and a woman together to honour God. We celebrate marriage for the way it brings a man and a woman together in God's name.

The call to the Christian marriage is a call which requires both husband and wife to open their heart as well as an inquiring mind to study the Bible together. The call to the Christian marriage is that, when a man and a woman discover Jesus as the Person to whom the entire Scripture points, then they must both respond to Him and worship God through Him alone.

The call to the Christian institution of marriage is a call specifically to glorify the name of God through marriage. The call to the institution of the Christian marriage is a call to use the Christian marriage as a means to evangelise the world. The call to the Christian institution of marriage involves a call to fellowship with God through Jesus Christ. The Call to the institution of the Christen marriage involves a call to two people travelling under the same banner and moving consistently towards the same goal.

The Christian marriage is a call to marriage pilgrimage, which requires, discipline, organization, faith, and vision. The call is to have a goal that should move Christians towards their objective. This objective must not permit them to allow any separation. The call to the Christian institution is a call to move ahead with the word of God, which is the light and glory of God until death separates them. The call to the institution of the Christian marriage is a call of being specific and objective. They are to dedicate themselves and the marriage supremely to its achievement.

Being a Christian couple involves very sobering responsibilities in moving the direction of the marriage towards God objective for His children. The call to the Christian institution of marriage involves bringing glory to God through their behaviour. The truth of the call to the institution of the Christian marriage is for God's purpose to be realized under the conditions mentioned by Paul in Ephesians 5:22-33.

God uses people who dedicate themselves and their marriage to Him as an instrument to bear His message of Salvation to the world. Are you the married couple God is looking for? The institution of Christian marriage is a covenant and comes with blessing available on the basis of faithfulness of the marriage. The call to the institution of the Christian marriage is a call to good moral values, behaviour and attitude and to be separated to God for service in the world.

THE NATURE OF THE CHRISTIAN MARRIAGE: We will now emphasize the fact that the institution of Christian marriage is a divine institution with a divine foundation of love. The Christian marriage is a divine institution established by God, therefore the Christian marriage has divine characteristics and purpose which lift it higher than any other marriage institution.

What does the foundation of a building do? It supports the rest of the building. The foundation holds the building up against beating elements such as wind and rain. The bodies of Christian couple are God's temple and His Spirit dwells in them, therefore a married couple must not engage in any immoral practices that will defile their body and their marriage. Such defilement will bring about God's judgement (1 Corinthians 3:7). Rather, we are exhorted to present our bodies as living sacrifices, holy and pleasing to God (Romans 12). In this way, we will fit into the spiritual building God is constructing in a beautiful, harmonious way. We will not attempt to force ourselves into God's structure to achieve our own selfish ways.

In 2 Corinthians 11:2-3, the apostle Paul uses the church to illustrate marital relations. The bride symbol speaks of the intimate union and the tender relationship between God and His people. God requires absolute loyalty and devotion. Similarly, in the Christian marriage, loyalty and devotion must be its banner. Any change in devotion and loyalty is a sin against God who instituted marriage.

Paul's use of the symbol (Ephesians 5:22-23) clearly speaks about the moral purity require in "marriage." In a Christian marriage, spouses must be committed unconditionally to the marriage. The Purity of a Christian wife flows out of her loyalty to her husband, in the same way the purity of the Christian husband flows out of his loyalty to his wife. However, if purity is not accompanied by love, it is empty.

There is no perfection in the Christian marriage; however, with the Holy Spirit's help we can make progress toward perfection. The call to the Christian marriage is a call to let the world know that God is a holy God and His children who are married must endeavour to keep their marriage holy to the glory of God.

Christian couples are called into marriage to demonstrate the practicality of the gospel. The Bible says, "Live such a good life among pagans that though they may accuse you of doing wrong, they may see your good work and glorify God (1 Peter 2:12). The Christian married couple must be aware nonbelievers watch the way they live their married lives, both in the home and outside the home, to see if their married live matches the Word of God. Consistent married Christian living before the world makes a powerful impression on nonbelieving married couples. Such examples are often a means of preparing their heart for the gospel message. As Christians, our married lives proclaim the very gospel we believe.

The call to the Christian married life is to demonstrate that Christian principles of behaviour can and should operate on a higher and better lever than those on which non-Christian marriage behaviour operates. Our obedience to the Word of God and our faithfulness to our marriage demonstrate not only that Christian principles are effective, but also that they work in our married lives.

As married Christian couples, it is only by living our married lives as children of the light that people of the world will see the correlation between our message and our attitude towards our spouse. What we do in our marital home and outside our marital home flows out of what we are. The call to a good Christian married life means that whole-hearted dedication is an absolute prerequisite for God's blessing in the marriage.

Warning: When an evil influence from people outside the marital home enters the heart of married couples, it forms an internal opposition that is subtle and hard to overcome that can only lead to the fire of love in the marriage being put out. Coldness towards our spouse is a step towards open opposition to our marriage. We must resist the temptation to become cold towards our spouse.

The Christian marriage is a divine institution in the midst of an evil and morally deprived world. The devil is always ready to offer married Christians a strong justification for him or her to accommodate the world's value and the standard of a nonbeliever's way of living their married life. Some married Christian have conformed to the world and lost their distinctive witness for Christ.

As the believer's marriage undergoes trial, he or she must draw close to God if he is to experience victory. The closer he draws, the more he sees what needs to be surrendered and committed to the loving heavenly father. However, the process of full surrender is not an easy one. Surrender of one's self to the Spirit's control means that one must crucify all of the insistent demands of the physical body and mind that create problems in the marriage. Through the daily experience of facing issues of marital life, the demands of the flesh, and the need to present our life as living sacrifices, the believer should endeavour to keep his or her life pure for God and for the marriage.

The call to the Christian marriage is also a call to have and use certain things that are in the world, but our love must be reserved for God and our marriage. The world by contrast, tends to use people and love things. We are to reverse this materialistic mindset in our devotion to Jesus Christ. It is absolutely essential that every believer meet successfully the world's challenge by overcoming the desires of the sinful nature.

Finally, may we respond obediently to the Spirit's call to the institution of the Christian marriage and be among those whom our Lord says, "Well done," because we were responsible for keeping the lamp of the Christian marriage burning and shining for the glory of God. However those whose action puts the burning flame out will have to answer for their actions someday.

Grandfather once said, "Those who forget history are likely to repeat the mistakes of the past." Today many Christians are involve in cross-cultural marriage for the wrong reasons, and as such are repeating history. The very reason that led to the floods does not appear to have sunk deep into the heart of some Christians because some Christians regard the account of the floods as a fairytale.

A good marriage requires the determination to be married for good. To make a marriage last will take work, love, patience, devotion, self-control, wise counselling of Christian friends, families and prayer. Above all, including God in decision-making is a vital principle for a marriage to be successful. How sad that bad counselling and keeping God out of our decision-making is what often set us apart from the person we so love and cherish.

Grandmother once told me that, marriage is like building and its survival depends on its foundation. History has taught us that the rise and fall of nations depends on a strong leadership and how the leaders run the affairs of that country. Similarly, for a marriage to survive storms will depend on how its foundation was build.

If courting couples build their marriage on a weak foundation it will crumble under the slightest storm. A good marriage depends on whether its foundation was build on Biblical principle or on worldly values. Every Christian marriage needs a good foundation for the marriage to stand on. A failed Christian marriage indicates there was something seriously wrong during the courting. The most possible reasons why there are many failed Christian marriages could be due to thee following reasons;

1. Weak marriage foundation.
2. Emphases were not placed on biblical principles.
3. Biblical principles are being compromised.

There is a Ghanaian proverb that says; "If a market will assume its supremacies signs of it are seen in the morning." Whatever goes wrong in a marriage can be traced back to the courting time. Compromising on Biblical principles releases a wave of storms in marriage. Therefore, young married couples are well advised to be on the look out for cracks in the marriage foundation.

When Christian courting couples behave like nonbelievers during courting by not living by Biblical principles the marriage often sink deeper into spiritual darkness. Bad Christian marriage often begins during courting because some Christian courting couples turn to drift away from Biblical principles towards worldly values. When courting couple's activities are not Christ-centred and filled with a sense of His purpose during courting the marriage becomes a mere human relationship and is spiritually dead.

The Biblical bases for the Christian marriage foundation are not human; they are divine. These bases are for greater love for God and for each other. The most important factor in the foundation of the Christian marriage is *divine enablement.* However, married couple must be responsive to the direction the Lord wants the marriage to go.

The Christian marriage is built on faith in the power of God rather than in the wisdom of men. In marriage, human ability alone is not a criterion suitable to be used as bases for a successful Christian marriage. But when we combine our human abilities and our spiritual gifts together God uses them to bless our marriage.

For a house to withstand adverse whether conditions the house must have a good foundation. Jesus Christ used the building of a house to illustrate the Kingdom of God when He told his audience that; "Therefore everyone who hears these words of mine and puts them into practice is like a wise man who built his house on the rock. The rain came down, and the streams rose, and the winds blew and beat against that house; yet it did not fall, because it had its foundation on the rock. But everyone who hears these words of mine and does not put them into practice is like a foolish man who built his house on the sand. The rain came down, the streams rose, and the winds blew and beat against that house, and it fell with a great crash." (Matthew 7:24-27).

When a marriage is built on Biblical principles they withstand storms and trials unleashed by the devil. A marriage that has its foundation built on Biblical principles from the very beginning can weather through every storm because its foundation rest on Biblical principles. Therefore, everyone who is called by the name of the LORD should build their marriage foundation Biblical principles.

When courting couples fail to use Biblical principles as building materials they are bound to face problems when storms begin to blow over the marriage. It very important for courting couples to know that the devil is always ready to offer a strong justification for us to accommodate ourselves to the world's values and relative standards of nonbelievers.

In marriage, Biblical principles are like a ring of fire that melts every element of trails that comes in contact with the marriage. Biblical principles are also like a defensive wall that protects the marriage from storms that beat against it.

Scripture does not give us a precise statement of the model of the Christian marriage. Nevertheless, it does give sets of clearly defined statement and goals, or list of qualifications, or standards against which one may gauge his or her marriage performance. However, we do find are patterns, examples, and objectives that when used can give us a composite picture of a model of the Christian marriage.

The Christian marriage is a divine institution with a divine foundation. It is an institution established by God Himself. The Christian marriage is an institution with a divine characteristic and purpose to lift it higher than any other religious or worldly marriage. The Christian marriage is suppose to develop into a radiant marriage, without stains and must be holy and blameless.

THINGS TO AVOID

The family is the most fundamental of the three institutions ordained by God: the family, the state and the Church. Everything which invades the sanctity of the home or minimizes its importance by undermining its authority endangers our whole Christian civilization.

The account of the creation of Eve clearly teaches that the body of the first woman was formed from that of the first man. When God created Eve, Adam perceives her at once to be "bone of my bone." Thus they became "one flesh" in that conjugal relationship which God has ordained for the comfort and happiness of mankind and the continuance of the race.

Marriage was instituted by God as the bond that brought man and woman together in solidarity. They were perfectly suited for each other's welfare and exclusive devotion to one another. Nonetheless, sex was God's gift to Adam and Eve, and is intended for their mutual enjoyment. Sex has been the way in which humans have most often attempted to usurp God's authority. **Outside marriage, sex destroys relationships. Within marriage, it is God's way of building a relationship** (1 Corinthians 10:13). Sexual temptations are difficult to withstand because they appeal to our normal and natural God- given desires. But God has assured us we will not be tempted beyond our ability to resist, with the help of his Holy Spirit (1 Corinthians 10:13).

The Seventh Commandment: "Thou shall not commit adultery." This commandment deals with the greatest menace to the home. Strictly interpreted, the word "adultery" means the violation of the exclusive right of the husband to the affection of his wife. Its primary aim is to prevent a married woman from bearing to her husband children that are not his. By implication it forbids "unchaste thoughts, word and actions" that the mutual love of husband and wife should be made the figure and type of the relationship between God and His people. Hosea 2:19, Ephesians 5:21-33 and other passages in the Bible give us the best possible illustrations of the ideal marriage. The prevalence of divorce and the ease, with which it can be obtained, are the greatest perils of the modern world. A husband or wife should never choose gratification of physical desires above the family. Let me sound this warning by making it clear that, "Thou shall not commit adultery," is one of the **Divine Absolute.** Breaking this commandment comes with grave consequences. This should give us a reason to keep away from any appearance of anything that could draw as closer to sin.

Today, God wants Christians to enjoy sex within the confines of marriage. Sex remains part of God's good creation, as a blessing for those who live in faithful, monogamous relationships. We might think of it as God's special wedding gift. But as with any of God's gifts, sexuality becomes tainted if we misuse it. The Scripture's guidelines on sex are meant to protect us from misusing God's gift and abusing each other.

Premarital and extramarital sex hurt us and compounds the effect of sin in our lives. God's grace can forgive and heal, but the consequences of sexual sin can last a lifetime. Human sexuality is not merely for reproduction, or even a means for expressing human passion. It is all of this, and more. Human sexuality in God's order becomes an instrument for covenantal blessing, both in one's relationship with God and with one's partner. In Genesis sex is elevated to an

233

expression of and commitment between a man and a woman who are mutually and exclusively devoted to each other.

Polygamy in the Bible: Polygamy, or the practice of having more than one spouse at the same time, was not God's ideal plan for marriage. The Scriptures clearly sanction marriage as the union of one man one woman (Genesis 2:18, 24). In the New Testament, Jesus confirmed this as the legitimate form of marriage (Mt. 19:4-6). Yet Scriptures nowhere specifically condemns polygamy. Instead, it often narrates the unfortunate effects of the practice. The first polygamist, Lamech, was a ruthless man (Genesis. 4:19-24). Jacob had two wives and two concubines. It was through this multiple marriage that God blessed the patriarchal family and began to fulfil his promises to multiply the descendants of Abraham. But the family was also rife with favouritism, deception, jealousy and betrayal (Genesis 25:28; 27:1-45; 35:22; 38:18-28).

Some of the future kings of Israel would also have more than one wife, but always with dreadful consequences: David (2 Samuel 3:2-5; 13:129; 15:18-33) and especially Solomon (1 Kings 11:1-4). Abraham and Hagar are unique because of the cultural parallels, and their relationship may not strictly be considered polygamy. Yet it, too had negative consequences (Genesis 16:4-16).

MARRIAGE = Intimacy or Isolation; Time when people realized they are in love. But when do we realise we are in love, to answer this question we need to understand what the word intimacy stands for. For the purpose of this book, intimacy can be defined as, loving relationships and emotional closeness between a man and a woman.

Raymond T. Brock in his book Introduction to Psychology: A Christian Perspective, stated the following; "Success in achieving intimacy represents the capacity to commit oneself to others. It includes but is not limited to sexual intimacy."

Why do people marry? Is it for intimacy or companionship? Could it for reason not mentioned here? A world in which people marry for personal reasons is a fertile ground for some to hide the truth and present lies as facts. Men and women in this category are likely to marry for their own selfish interest. Failure to achieve intimacy can lead to isolation and isolation leads to depression in which intimacy is avoided and character problems develop.

Sexual promiscuity develops when a person separates sex from love and avoids commitment in interpersonal relationships. When the person who moves into isolation repudiates life and seeks not to accept any relationship, he or she becomes enveloped in a cloud of darkness. This happens when people do not want to relate to each other. Some people might not want to relate to others because of shyness, worries, depressions, distrust, fear or anxiety. Fear and anxiety can rob a person of joy and peace. Fear can cause physical problems such as headaches, heart attacks, increased blood pressure and lack of sleep.

Marriage is not necessarily an indication that intimacy has been achieved. A common misconception about marriage is that it is the solution to loneliness. Marriage does not solve the problem of loneliness. Those who think intimacy is a way out of loneliness will find their heart filled with emptiness if can only be filled by Jesus Christ.

Today many young men and women rush into marriage without understanding its ethics, only to discover that they have made the wrong decision or the wrong choice. Some young people get married just to get away from home, only to discover that they are confronted with the another unhappiness. Individuals who married to solve their problems of loneliness or sexuality often discover they are locked in an unhappy union. This is the underlying cause of divorce in so many marriages. In some marriages, it is evident that when intimacy has not been achieved, the people involved become lonely.

Do not marry because friends are getting married. You must marry for the right reasons and when the conditions for marriage are right for you. We must only marry when we are spiritually and physically ready; and the person we are about to marry must also be spiritually and physically ready. It is evident that women are usually mentally and physically ready and prepared for marriage than men of the same age. Women usually want to get married younger than men. This is so because of the nature of women: women tend to mature faster than their male counterparts.

Women also come under strong pressure from family and friends to get married much more so than men. This could be a contributing factor to early marriage for women. While women think and worry about getting married, men think and worry about being financially sound and prepared before thinking of getting married.

SOLVING PROBLEM

Grandmother once said; *"Marriage is a choice between obeying the marriage vows and stubbornly disobeying it. A spouse who disobeys his marriage vows is a like a horse which has no understanding and must be harnesses to be brought under control."* Tragically this is the behaviour of some people in marriage. We must see grandmother's words as a challenge and then ponder over what pattern we want to choose. Obeying your marriage vows will lead to a happy and successful marriage life, and disobeying it will ultimately break your marriage.

There are two kinds of people in any marriage. 1. Those who buy a single flight ticket into the marriage and 2, those who buy a return ticket into the marriage. You will never know the difference between them until things begins to go wrong and the toxic that has been lying dormant begins to spew its deadly cargo of toxic material.

1. **Those who buy a single flight ticket into marriage** are those who go into marriage determined to work hard toward its success, no matter the storms. Those in this group don't wait until they are overwhelmed by problems in the marriage but stop them before it happens. When trouble shows its ugly head they are quick to discern where the trouble is coming from and then deal with it before it gains root. Those in this group are unmovable by marriage storms because they want to be part of the marriage success story. They are very understanding, very

caring, very forgiving and above all understand what it means to be married to the person they have married. They do not run away from marital storms but confront the problem peacefully. They know marital problem has two sources; spiritual or physical. This gives them a head-start on the problem. A married person with the ability to discern the source of the problems in the marriage is well-placed and equipped to deal with the issue in the marriage. They seek the highest interest of their spouse. Seeking the highest interest of your spouse is like a spiritual sword with which you can fight the problem and a shield with which you can defend yourself from the poisonous arrows shot from outside the marriage. They know marital problems are not fought with the power of words but with patience, staying calm even when annoyed, without fighting back.

2. **Those who buy a return flight ticket into marriage:** They are usually unstable in the marriage because go into marriage with an exit visa containing a map and direction on how to exit the marriage quickly when problems start. They cannot withstand constant quarrelling in the marriage. They simply do not have the stomach for marriage troubles. What they don't know is that every marriage has its problem and those who join the institution of marriage must be prepared for it. There is no perfect marriage because human nature is not perfect. People who come into marriage with the notion that when things are not working as expected then the only solution is to walkout should be informed that marriage is not a trouble-free institution. We don't run away from marriage problems but we

confront them with the weapons of love, patience and self-control, unless we are in danger. People in this group go into marriage looking back because they know they have a **return ticket.** And this is bad for the marriage institution. Good and successful marriages do not come easy but through hard work and with the weapons of patience, understanding and forgiveness.

When things begin to go wrong in the marriage to whom do you turn? The safest rule in such circumstances is to:

1. **Remain steadfast:** In your love, faithfulness and loyalty to your spouse. The ongoing storm in the marriage should not make you waver about your feelings toward your spouse. Under no circumstances should you draw conclusion on what you have heard and yet have not seen. Your spouse may be going through emotional stress that could be work-related or from within the marriage. There is also the possibility that what caused the stress could be an extended family problem. Besides, the daily stresses of life can easily cause us to get irritable with our spouses and pick at the littlest annoyance or criticise minor habits. This makes us blurt out harmful, unkind words with to spouse.

2. **Self-Control:** The ability to remain calm and not show your emotions even though you are feeling angry. We must not let ourselves be overcome by emotions because what is happening may only be temporary. If you allow your emotions to control you, you will be acting irrationally. It does sometimes happen in marriage to find your spouse's behaviour very strange. In marriage, the

ability for us to remain calm in the midst of a highly-charged situation and not show any signs of bitterness, even though we are angry, holds the power to defuse the problem.

3. **Communication:** The way and manner we communicate during our anger can either inflame the situation or bring about a lasting peace in the marriage. Communication can either lead to further misunderstanding or understanding. When some people are very upset they speak before they think and this can be damaging. An effective manner of communication like choice of words, use of words or the manner we frame sentences can bring about healing in our marriage. The use of offensive language during arguments is very bad for marriage. The following are the words of a wise preacher; "Pleasant words are a honeycomb, sweet words to the soul and healing to the bones" (Proverbs 16:24). The book gives us counsel about the words we use to others. It says, "Whoever guards his mouth and tongue keeps his soul from troubles" (21:23). There are these warnings: "Death and life are in the power of the tongue" (18:21); and "Reckless words pierce like a sword, but the tongue of the wise brings healing." (12:18). *"The Lord detests lying lips, but he delights in men who are truthful"* (Proverbs 12:22).

4. **Forgiveness:** Is one of the foundations of marriage. Forgiveness is like the spinal-cord that keeps us walking upright. When the spinal-cord is severed we lose the use of our legs and several part of our body. Similarly, without forgiveness marriage breaks apart. Forgiveness is what keeps marriage going. If marriage has legs to walk on

then these legs are forgiveness. If a marriage can no longer walk then its spinal-cord, "forgiveness" has been severed. Every two in three marriages that break down are due to spouses' unwillingness to forgive. The compass needle in every marriage points to forgiveness. If that compass needle in the marriage points to any other direction the marriage will be heading toward divorce. When the compass needle in marriage is pointing towards forgiveness then the marriage will succeed. Cohesiveness in marriage is the result of the marriage compass pointing to forgiveness. Every successful marriage's compass needle always points to forgiveness. A preacher once wrote the following wise saying; "A man's wisdom gives him patience; it is to his glory to overlook an offence." (Proverbs 19:11)

5. **For the peace and welfare of the home it is important for the husband and wife to observe the following rules:** (a) Keep lines of communication open. There must be a constant readiness to talk things out. When steam is allowed to build up in the boiler, an explosion is inevitable. Talking things out includes the willingness for each to say, "I am sorry" "I forgive". (b) Maintain absolute honesty in order to have a basis of mutual confidence.

6. **Faults:** Overlook minor faults and idiosyncrasies. Don't demand perfection in others when you are unable to produce it yourself.

7. **Finance:** Avoid overspending, instalment buying, buy today and pay tomorrow and the lust to keep up with your friends.

8. **The Dangerous Tongue:** when we are facing severe trials and suffering in our marriage, the

last thing we need is a set of "Job's counsellors," people who only tell us what they think we have done wrong. Rather than having people on our back, we would prefer people who are on our team, pulling for us as we wrestle with our problems. In time of marital problems we all need a shoulder to cry on. But the question is on whose shoulder are you going to lean on in times of storms in the marriage? In times of marital storms so many things run through our mind. If you are not very careful you would end up making one mistake after the other. The warning is that there are so many itching ears and people whose mouths are full of deadly poison.

The difference between a compliment and flattery is often motive. A compliment offers genuine appreciation of action seen in another person. The goal of flattery is usually self- advancement through gaining the favour of someone else. Compliment seeks to encourage; while flattery attempts to manipulate. If God controls our lips then our speech will mirror His words, which David described as "pure words, like silver tried in a furnace of earth, purified seven times" (Psalm 12:6).

James the brother Jesus wrote the following to his Jewish audience and has this to say about the tongue and what it can do to your marriage. *"Likewise the tongue is a small part of the body, but it makes great boast. Consider what a great forest is set on fire by a small spark. The tongue also is a fire, a small world of evil among the parts of the body. It corrupts the whole person, sets the whole course of his life on fire, and it itself set on fire by hell. All kinds of animals, birds, reptiles and creatures of the sea are being tamed and have been tamed by man, but no man can tame the tongue. It is a restless evil, full of deadly poison. With the tongue we praise our Lord and Father, and with it we curse men, who have been made in God's likeness. Out of the same mouth comes praising and cursing.* (James 3:5-9)

What does the apostle James means by his inspired words above? I think what he wants to put across is the abuse of the tongue by both Christians and unbelievers. The way we use the tongue can result in the murder of innocent people. If you note carefully you will find that the first twelve verses of chapter 3 deal with the tongue.

Here James challenges every believer to test their spiritual health by the way of their conversation. Self-diagnosis begins with sin speech. The way we talk reveals our faithfulness and obedience to the Word of God. Grandmother once said, "The way we talk about others reveals the kind of God we worship." This sums up James warning how to curb our tongue and live our life for the glory of God.

This is what grandfather once told me, "The Holy Spirit is what controls and put limits on our tongue." It is only when we learn how to control our tongue that we can become effective ambassadors of Christ. The fact is that we all are prone to stumble in many ways, but if we can control our tongue then those who look to us can see the beauty of Christ. The tongue can defile the whole body. A person can corrupt his whole personality by using his tongue to slander, abuse, lie, blaspheme, and swear.

Some marriages break down because of what we tell outsider about our marriage. Troubled marriages that should never have gone through the divorce court have ended in divorce because we could not tame our tongue. When marriages are going through troubled times those who were not part of the problem can never be a solution.

Grandmother once said "No matter the storms in a marriage we should never disclose anything in the marriage to outsiders. And whatever goes on in the marriage must remain under lock and key and nothing is leaked out." She said the day you leak any information to anyone because you feel you can trust that person could worsen the problem, except when you are suffering from domestic abused."

Storms in the marriage are for the husband and wife to deal with and not to seek assistance from outside the marriage. You may ask why. The answer lies in the poisonous tongue which cannot be tamed. You tell Laura the pastor's wife a little bit of your problem, she then tells her trusted friend Dorothy; " The trouble here is that Dorothy also has a trusted friend called Ruth. Ruth also has trusted friend to whom she can confine her secrets. The link of confiding secrets becomes endless. Sooner or later the little information you leaked out would spread like wildfire. Remember what the apostle James said, "No man has been able to tame the tongue."

The action of the pastor's wife reminds me of what grandfather once told me about gossip. He said, "Gossip is like a man who on a windy day took a pillow full of cotton and climbs on top of a mountain and started emptying cotton out of the pillow case. Then after emptying half of the content he realised he made a mistake and wanted to collect what he had thrown away back into the pillow case. To retrieve what he had dispensed would be an impossible task. This is what gossipers are like. For the pastor's wife it is the diet of constant gossip that fed her fascination with gossip. Christians who feed on a constant diet of gossip are no friend of Jesus. A pastor's wife keeps confidences. One of the most important and necessary characteristics for both the pastor and his wife is that they never repeat any confidential matters that people share with them.

Grandmother once said, "The more a Christian focus his mind on heaven, the more gossip becomes unattractive to him, similarly the more the Christian takes his mind away from heaven, the more gossip become attractive to him." Gossip separates the best of friends and sets a brother against a brother and a sister against a sister. God's presence with us is His greatest present to us that can set us free the sin of gossip.

King Solomon said that speaking badly of others (gossip) could have a disastrous effect on them. Besides, it betrays the confidence they have in you. Gossip can separate close friends. Gossip does not build bridges; rather it destroys the foundation of bridges. Gossip fuels quarrels and destroys relationships. Damage done by gossip can be irreparable because it leaves lasting pain.

Let the Lord help us to not engage in harmful talk about other people's marriage. God wants us to set a guard over our mouth so that we will instead speak all the good we know about everybody. Do not turn your mouth into breeding ground for gossip; rather let what comes out of your mouth be a blessing to those who need a blessing and healing for those who need healing, and finally a restoration for those whose marriages are going through difficulties and needs comfort and restoration.

A family friend's wife once went to her pastor for counselling on an ongoing issue in the marriage. Her husband wanted them to resolve the issue themselves but the wife spoke to her pastor without her husband's approval. The husband who was not a member of the Church the wife went for the counselling visited the church one Sunday morning without telling his wife. The unfortunate thing was that what this man's wife discussing with her pastor became the subject of the sermon that day. Halfway through the sermon the pastor noticed the husband sitting among the congregation.

The shellshock husband sat down and marvelled how the pastor could explain so vividly the ongoing marital problem in the family that he thought no one knew except his wife. This man walked out of the church disappointed and never to trust his wife again. As for the pastor, he lost his credibility before some members of the congregation.

In his book, (A Guide to Practical Christian living) based on (James 1:26), Adrian Rogers wrote the following about Christians who cannot bridle their tongue, "What kind of religion do you practice? What would happen if your family, neighbour, and co-workers testified about you? Have they witnessed a sold-out life for Christ? Or do you just "seem" to be religious?" If you are, then one way you will know it, James says, is by the way you speak.

Nothing can do more damage to the cause of Christ and the glory of our Lord than people who seem to be religious and yet don't bridle their tongue. Do you know anyone like that? Perhaps you've been hurt by a Christian who has talked behind your back? You may be a Church member and baptized, but if you are slanderer, liar, or gossip then you need to ask God for His mercy to convict you and bring you to repentance."

What you may not be aware of is that most marriages break down as a result of information in our marriage that we disclose to outsiders. The discloser of such information gives greater opportunity for people who envy your marriage to come in and light a fire under the already melting thin ice on which your marriage now stands on.

The best rule in marriage is that in times of trouble marriage storms; **Say nothing, Reveal nothing, Confined in no one and trust no one except God.** But people who cannot handle storms become disoriented and give away clues that will help destroy their marriage and at the end become disillusioned at the very people they hold in confidence. Marriage problems must never go beyond the marital home.

What we don't know is that Satan and his team of marriage wreckers have no ideal of what goes on in our marriage unless we disclose such vital information to them. It is what we feed them with from our marriage they use to destroy our marriage. Your enemy does not know your weak point so he can't destroy you.

Only Jesus, who calmed the storm when His disciples were faced with danger while they were in the boat can calm the storm in your marriage when you confide in Him.

A pamphlet was once dropped through my letter box; the pamphlet contained ten point of information given by the police on how to keep burglars out of you home. One of the listed points that caught my attention was where it stated: "When away, keep all curtains drawn so that the burglar will not know there is no one at home." When we leave our curtains open, it give burglars the opportunity to see what would interest him in our home.

Marriage is like that. Marriage wreckers don't know what goes on behind the drawn curtain except we open up by telling what interest them. The safest rule is to keep your martial curtains drawn at all times so that marriage wreckers will have nothing to see. When marriage wreckers **do not see, don't hear and don't smell what goes on in your marriage they will have nothing to talk about and nothing to feed on.**

Doesn't the Scripture warn us not to trust any man except God? So why are you desperate to pass on vital information about the weakness in your marriage to an enemy you see as a friend? Mother once said; "If you know who your enemies are, then your marriage will be rock solid and unmovable by marriage wreckers." Marriages break down because we draw back the marital curtain to reveal things for gossipers.

In a marriage where there is constant physical abuse it is best to seek a temporary sanctuary somewhere until you are certain such physical violence will not continue. If your spouse is a violent person and does not show any sign of willing to change then be bold and tell him or her, "Enough is enough, you better stop the beating or the marriage is over." In stormy marriages there are several options available for the one being abused to take. 1. If you are both Christian and attend the same church report him to the pastor without delay. 2. If you attend different church then report him to his pastor. 3. Report to his father or mother. 4. Seek the help of a married Christian counsellor. 5. Look for a temporary shelter with either his parents or your parents. 6. Look for a temporary shelter with a friend you know can't influence you or make you to walk out of the marriage. 7. If he is a violent husband, look for a temporary home where he can never find you until the problem are resolved. 8. Do not go back to your marital home until you can trust that you will be safe in the house. 9. While all this is going on you must spend time in fasting and prayers for his deliverance. 10. If you have children take them with you. There are also N. G. Os' which offer temporary shelter and help for battered women you can run to for help while your problems are being dealt with by the experts.

There are some difficult problems in marriage that are best left for God to deal with. Usually such problems are more spiritual than physical. The details of spiritual problems that have ravaged marriages can be found in my book, '**The Praying Husband.**' It unearths all what we need to know about spiritual marriage problems. It is futile confronting spiritual things with what is physical.

From the beginning, it has been the wish of God who instituted the marriage institution that all married couples will live together until death separates them. God never intended that marriages should end in divorce. That is why He provided everything we need to make marriage to work in the Scriptures. Today, ninety five percent of what causes divorce is **disagreement.** All marriages break down because the two people in the marriage cannot **agree.**

God in His word through the prophet Amos said: "**Do two walk together unless they have agreed to do so?**" (Amos 3:3). The cause of every marriage break-down has to do with disagreement between the couple over issues.

Grandmother once said, "In every marriage one of them has to behave like a fool for the sake of peace to prevail in the home. This does not mean the one who has chosen to behave like a fool is really a fool. Two wise people cannot live in the same marriage; it is often the wisest person in the marriage who chooses to behave like a fool for the sake of harmony."

It is difficult for two wise married couple to agree over an issue when they both chose to hold their ground. This is where the wisest person between the two plays the fool because of his or her love for the other. It is love that binds her to her husband or to his wife that makes him or her play the fool so that peace will prevail in the home.

There is no perfect marriage because no man or woman can be perfect. This is the reason why there is no perfection in marriage. Even men of God who are suppose to know better and set a good example in marriage for believers and unbeliever are themselves found wanting because they cannot hold their marriage together.

In times of sudden storms in marriage, spouses must never start blaming the guilty spouse rather he or she must be compassionate toward the guilty one and be willing to forgive. Blaming him or her and resurrecting all that he or she has done in the past will only worsen the situation and lead to retribution.

If a person thinks he or she is mature enough to marry then they must exercise maturity in marriage when it comes to resolving problems. Understanding is the key in solving some of the problem in marriage. Our ability to reason that we are all prone to error will bring us to the place of understanding which will lead to healing.

Grandmother once said this, "Avoid people who advice you to walk out of your marriage, unless the situation is life-threatening." People who advice you to walk out of your marriage are not always good friends. Marriage its self is a bond of love between two people who seek each other's highest interest to the exclusion of all others. Married couple who seek each others interest are very understanding and forgiving. You cannot seek your spouse's highest interest and not be willing to forgive him or her for whatever they might have done. Understanding and the willingness to forgive holds the key to a successful marriage. Successful marriage does not come without the following:

1. **Sacrifice:** In marriage it involves burying our pride, what you value as important in your life and sometimes our rights if it will lead to peace.

Sometimes it involves being silent when we feel we should be talking. It also involves doing what we think we should not be doing. Sacrifice covers all areas of marriage.

2. **Hard Work:** A successful marriage does not come without hard work. In marriage it involves dedicating your entire life to the marriage. You cannot go into marriage half-hearted and expect to be successful. Marriage does not work that way. There is no place for selfishness in marriage. Sometimes it involves staying up all night planning how to succeed in the marriage. Hard work involves being well organized in the day-to-day work in the home, setting targets and working to meet them.

3. **Understanding:** Marriage has no place for people with a temperamental heart. People with such a heart condition must first deal with it before even thinking of going into marriage. One of the qualities of a successful marriage is understanding your spouse. The ability to understand why your spouse is behaving in manner that is contrary to what the institution of marriage regards as the norm will help you to be understanding. For example, your spouse has taken to drinking heavily which you find yourself unable to cope with. Your loving spouse has suddenly turned alcoholic, something he never did when you were dating. Situation like this calls for understanding and finding out the reasons behind the sudden behaviour. Or your spouse has turned you into a punching bag. An extreme negative reaction towards your spouse will worsen or will inflame the situation. What you must understand is that your spouse needs help and not a negative reaction that will derive

him or her out of the marital home. When we fail to understand why some people's behaviour is out of character, it creates storms in our own life.

4. **Forgiveness:** Marriage breaks down because spouses are unwilling to forgive. This is the reason why we have so many divorces in our society today. Every two in three marriages that break down are because spouses are unwilling to forgive. When two people are unwilling to forgive no one can help them. People who are unwilling to forgive have already made up their minds to walk out of the marriage. For a marriage to be successful there has to be forgiveness. Someone in the marriage has to swallow his or pride and say **I am very sorry** before he or she can be forgiven. "**Without repentance there is no forgiveness.**" Marriage is about forgiveness because without forgiveness there cannot a successful marriage. Two imperfect people cannot go into marriage and be unwilling to forgive when things start going wrong. Imperfect spouses who expect their spouses to be perfect are looking for an apple in a citrus farm. As humans we all have our shortcoming, therefore we cannot expect to be in marriage and not willing to forgive. Forgiveness is the bedrock of marriage. You cannot expect a successful marriage without forgiveness. People who understand what it means to be married know what it means to forgive. You will be wasting your time fasting and praying if you don't know why you should forgive your spouse or can't bring yourself to forgive him or her. Marriages not built on the foundation of forgiveness will crumble when the foundation comes under intense pressure. For peace to reign

in the marital home there has to room for forgiveness. Forgiveness is **Divine Absolute.**

Never trust or depend on any person because human nature is very corrupt and prone to errors for Scripture says, **"Cursed is the one who trust in a man, who depend on the flesh for his strength and whose heart turns away from the LORD"** (Jeremiah 17:5). In marriage we all expect to have someone we can confide our problems to when things start going wrong. This is where the problems start. The more we realise the human nature is corrupt and imperfect the less we would confide things that should rather be left unsaid.

In this world, man is a creature of hope that lives for the future. Sometimes he is frustrated and looks forward for a better day only to find darkness and gloom, broken dreams, broken marriage and dashed hopes. In this life, the fulfilment of hope is never certain. But one day all the deepest desires and longings, all that is truly enjoyable, all that fully satisfies, will find their perfect fulfilment. At some appointed time known only by God, hope will become reality. Man's fellowship with God will be completely restored. One cannot imagine anything more joyful for God's redeemed people. For some married men and women the measure of their future usefulness and success to their marriage may depend on their answer to this question.

As married Christians God dwells in us, therefore, we must not engage in habits and practices that will defile our bodies. Such defilement will bring about God's judgement and ridicule from unbelievers. We are exhorted to present our bodies as living sacrifices, holy and pleasing to God (1 Corinthians 6:19 and 3:17). In this way we fit to be part of that divine institution.

Moral purity is required of both courting couples and married spouses. Married Christian spouses must be committed unconditionally to Christ, but devotion to purity should not be empty words. Purity in the Christian marriage flows out our devotion and loyalty to Christ. But if purity in our marriage is not accompanied by love then it is empty.